Gastronomic Delights

Exploring the World's Best Culinary Traditions

Camille Bates

Table of Contents

Chapter 1
Introduction to Gastronomy

The Evolution of Culinary Arts

The history of culinary arts is a rich tapestry woven from diverse cultures, traditions, and innovations. From the earliest days of human civilization, food preparation has evolved into a sophisticated discipline that reflects the social, economic, and technological changes of our times. Understanding this evolution provides insight into how culinary practices have shaped, and been shaped by, the world around us.

The story of culinary arts begins with the dawn of humanity. Early humans were hunter-gatherers, relying on the natural world for sustenance. Their diet consisted of raw fruits, vegetables, nuts, and meat scavenged from animal kills. The discovery of fire marked a pivotal moment in culinary history. Cooking not only made food more palatable but also unlocked nutrients that were previously inaccessible, fostering human development and social interaction. Around campfires, early humans shared cooked meals, which enhanced communal bonds and laid the groundwork for social structures.

As societies transitioned from nomadic to settled agricultural communities, the culinary arts began to flourish. The domestication of plants and animals allowed for a more stable food supply, leading to the development of early farming techniques. Ancient civilizations like Mesopotamia, Egypt, and the Indus Valley began to cultivate grains, fruits, and vegetables, and to raise livestock. These advances in agriculture were accompanied by innovations in food storage and preparation, including fermentation, drying, and salting.

In Ancient Egypt, food was a central part of religious rituals and daily life. The Egyptians developed advanced techniques for baking bread and brewing beer, staples of their diet. They also made use of a variety of spices and herbs to flavor their dishes, a practice that would become a hallmark of sophisticated cuisine. Tomb paintings and hieroglyphs provide detailed records of Egyptian culinary practices, revealing a diet rich in fruits, vegetables, fish, and meat.

The culinary traditions of Ancient Greece and Rome further advanced the art of cooking. The Greeks viewed food as an essential aspect of social and intellectual life. Symposia, or banquet gatherings, featured a variety of dishes and wines, accompanied by philosophical discussions and entertainment. Greek cuisine emphasized the use of fresh, local ingredients, and olive oil, honey, and wine were central to their diet.

The Romans, influenced by Greek culinary traditions, expanded their repertoire by incorporating foods and techniques from the far reaches of their empire. Roman feasts, known as convivium, were lavish affairs showcasing the wealth and power of the host. These meals featured multiple courses, including meats, seafood, fruits, and desserts, often prepared with intricate sauces and seasonings. The development of Roman cookbooks, such as Apicius's "De Re Coquinaria," underscores the importance of culinary arts in their society.

During the Middle Ages, the culinary arts were shaped by the feudal system and the influence of the Church. Monasteries became centers of agricultural and culinary innovation, with monks cultivating herbs, fruits, and vegetables, and brewing beer and wine. Medieval cuisine was characterized by the use of spices, which were highly prized and often imported from distant lands. The spice trade not only influenced European cuisine but also played a significant role in the exploration and colonization of new territories.

The Renaissance period marked a resurgence of interest in the culinary arts, driven by the revival of classical learning and the exchange of ideas between

Europe and the East. Italian cuisine, in particular, experienced a golden age, with the introduction of new ingredients such as tomatoes, potatoes, and maize from the Americas. The publication of cookbooks, such as Bartolomeo Scappi's "Opera dell'Arte del Cucinare," reflected the growing sophistication of Renaissance cooking and the emergence of professional chefs.

The 17th and 18th centuries saw the rise of French cuisine as a dominant force in the culinary world. The establishment of the French court at Versailles under Louis XIV created a demand for elaborate banquets and refined dishes. Chefs like François Pierre La Varenne and Marie-Antoine Carême revolutionized French cooking by codifying techniques and recipes, emphasizing the importance of sauces and presentation. The development of haute cuisine during this period set the standard for fine dining, with an emphasis on artistry and precision.

The Industrial Revolution brought about significant changes in the culinary arts. Advances in technology and transportation made a wider variety of ingredients available to cooks, and the rise of the middle class created a demand for more accessible and diverse food options. The invention of canning, refrigeration, and other preservation methods transformed food storage and distribution, making fresh produce and perishables more widely available.

The 20th century saw the globalization of culinary arts, with the exchange of culinary traditions across continents. Immigration and travel introduced new flavors and techniques to different parts of the world, leading to the fusion of cuisines. The rise of culinary schools and the professionalization of the culinary industry elevated the status of chefs and brought about a greater emphasis on culinary education and innovation.

In recent decades, the culinary arts have continued to evolve, driven by a growing interest in health, sustainability, and gastronomy. The farm-to-table movement emphasizes the use of fresh, locally sourced ingredients, while advancements in molecular gastronomy explore the science behind food preparation and presentation. The rise of food media, including television shows, blogs, and social media, has made culinary arts more accessible to the general public, inspiring home cooks and professional chefs alike.

Understanding Gastronomy

Gastronomy, at its core, is the art and science of good eating. It encompasses a broad range of activities, knowledge, and experiences related to food and drink. Understanding gastronomy requires a deep appreciation of the cultural, historical, and social contexts in which food is prepared and consumed. It's an exploration that goes beyond mere sustenance, delving into the intricate relationships between ingredients, techniques, and traditions that define culinary practices around the world.

To truly grasp the essence of gastronomy, one must first recognize its multifaceted nature. It's not just about cooking; it's about the entire process of food production, preparation, presentation, and consumption. This includes understanding the origins of ingredients, the methods used to cultivate and harvest them, and the ways in which they are transformed from raw materials into finished dishes. It's a holistic approach that considers the environmental, economic, and ethical implications of food choices.

One of the fundamental aspects of gastronomy is the concept of terroir. This French term refers to the unique combination of natural factors—such as soil, climate, and topography—that influence the characteristics of agricultural products. Terroir plays a crucial role in defining the flavors and qualities of foods and beverages, particularly in wine, cheese, and other artisanal products. For example, the distinct taste of a Burgundy wine is attributed to the specific conditions of the Burgundy region's vineyards. Understanding terroir helps us appreciate the diversity and complexity of flavors that different regions offer.

Seasonality is another key element in gastronomy. The best chefs and food enthusiasts emphasize the importance of using seasonal ingredients, which are fresher, more flavorful, and often more nutritious. This practice not only enhances the quality of dishes but also supports local farmers and reduces the environmental impact of transporting out-of-season produce across long distances. By aligning cooking with the natural cycles of growth and harvest, gastronomy fosters a deeper connection between people and the land.

Culinary techniques form the backbone of gastronomy. These methods, developed over centuries, range from basic skills like chopping and sautéing to advanced techniques such as sous-vide and molecular gastronomy. Each technique brings out different qualities in ingredients, affecting their texture, flavor, and appearance. Mastering these techniques requires both practice and an understanding of the science behind them. For instance, knowing how heat affects proteins and carbohydrates can help a cook achieve the perfect sear on a steak or the ideal caramelization on roasted vegetables.

Gastronomy also involves the art of food presentation. The visual appeal of a dish can significantly enhance the dining experience, making it more enjoyable and memorable. Plating techniques, the use of color and texture, and the arrangement of food on the plate all contribute to the overall aesthetic. This aspect of gastronomy highlights the creative side of cooking, where chefs can express their artistic vision and personal style.

Another important dimension of gastronomy is the cultural significance of food. Every cuisine reflects the history, geography, and values of the people who created it. Traditional dishes often tell stories of migration, trade, and adaptation, carrying with them the legacy of generations. For example, the spices used in Indian cuisine reflect centuries of trade with other regions, while the hearty stews of Eastern Europe tell of a history of agricultural communities. Understanding these cultural contexts enriches our appreciation of different cuisines and fosters a sense of global connectedness.

The social aspect of gastronomy cannot be overlooked. Food has always been a central element of human gatherings, from family meals to festive celebrations. Sharing a meal is a universal act of hospitality and community, transcending cultural and linguistic barriers. Gastronomy, in this sense, is also about the rituals and etiquettes associated with dining, which vary widely across cultures. Whether it's the Japanese tea ceremony or the Italian tradition of Sunday family dinners, these practices underscore the role of food in building and maintaining social bonds.

Modern gastronomy is increasingly concerned with issues of sustainability and ethics. As awareness of environmental and social issues grows, there is a greater emphasis on responsible sourcing and consumption. This includes supporting organic farming, reducing food waste, and promoting fair trade practices. Chefs and consumers alike are becoming more mindful of the impact of their food choices on the planet and on the people who produce and prepare their food. This shift towards sustainability is reshaping the culinary landscape, encouraging innovations that align with ecological and ethical values.

In addition to these broader themes, gastronomy also involves a personal journey of discovery and experimentation. For many, the kitchen is a place of creativity and exploration, where they can experiment with new ingredients and techniques, and develop their own recipes. This process is often guided by curiosity and a love of learning. Tasting new dishes, visiting different markets, and engaging with other food enthusiasts are all part of this gastronomic adventure. It's an ongoing process that invites individuals to expand their culinary horizons and deepen their understanding of food.

The role of education in gastronomy cannot be understated. Culinary schools, food writing, and cooking shows all contribute to the dissemination of knowledge and skills. They provide aspiring chefs and home cooks with the tools they need to elevate their culinary practice. Moreover, food education fosters a greater appreciation of the complexities and joys of cooking, encouraging more thoughtful and informed food choices.

Understanding gastronomy is also about recognizing its dynamic nature. As cultures evolve and interact, so too do their culinary traditions. Fusion cuisine, which combines elements from different culinary traditions, exemplifies this dynamic quality. It reflects the ongoing exchange of ideas and flavors, resulting in innovative and exciting new dishes. This adaptability ensures that gastronomy remains a vibrant and relevant field, constantly evolving to reflect contemporary tastes and values.

The Role of Gastronomy in Culture

Food is more than mere sustenance; it is a vibrant expression of culture, history, and identity. The role of gastronomy in culture is multifaceted, reflecting a society's values, traditions, and innovations. From festive feasts to everyday meals, the foods we eat and the ways we prepare them tell stories of who we are, where we come from, and how we see the world. Understanding this role requires a journey through time and across continents, exploring the intricate connections between culinary practices and cultural heritage.

One of the most profound ways gastronomy influences culture is through traditional cuisine. Every culture has its own unique set of dishes that have been passed down through generations. These recipes often use local ingredients and time-honored cooking methods, preserving the flavors and techniques of the past. For example, the intricate preparation of Japanese sushi, with its precise knife skills and careful selection of ingredients, reflects a deep respect for nature and craftsmanship. Similarly, the slow-cooked stews of rural France, such as Coq au Vin, showcase the importance of local produce and the communal aspect of food preparation.

Festivals and celebrations provide a vivid illustration of how gastronomy can encapsulate cultural identity. Around the world, food plays a central role in marking significant events and rituals. During Chinese New Year, families gather to prepare and share intricate dishes like dumplings and fish, symbolizing prosperity and reunion. In Mexico, the Day of the Dead is celebrated with offerings of food and drink for deceased loved ones, including traditional items like pan de muerto and sugar skulls. These culinary traditions are not just about eating; they are about honoring heritage and reinforcing community bonds.

Migration and globalization have further enriched the relationship between gastronomy and culture. As people move across borders, they bring their culinary traditions with them, creating a mosaic of flavors and techniques in their new homes. This blending of cuisines can lead to exciting innovations and the creation of entirely new culinary styles. The fusion cuisine of places like Singapore, where Chinese, Malay, Indian, and Western influences merge, is a testament to the dynamic interplay of food and culture. Such culinary exchanges foster greater cultural understanding and appreciation, breaking down barriers and building bridges between diverse communities.

Language and gastronomy are also deeply intertwined. The terminology and nomenclature used in cooking often reflect a culture's unique way of interacting with food. Italian cuisine, for instance, has a rich vocabulary to describe pasta shapes, each with its own regional variations and specific uses. In France, the language of cooking has been codified into a precise system, with terms like "mise en place" and "sauté" becoming universal in professional kitchens worldwide. These linguistic nuances not only facilitate the transmission of culinary knowledge but also reinforce cultural identity and pride.

The role of gastronomy in culture is also evident in the way societies adapt to changing circumstances through their culinary practices. Historical events, such as wars, colonization, and economic shifts, have often led to significant changes in what people eat and how they prepare food. The introduction of new ingredients, such as tomatoes, potatoes, and chilies to Europe following the Columbian Exchange, revolutionized European cuisines. These ingredients, once foreign, became staples in dishes like Italian pasta sauce and Spanish gazpacho, illustrating how cultures can absorb and transform external influences.

Religious beliefs and practices have a profound impact on gastronomy. Many religions have dietary laws and rituals that dictate what can be eaten, how it should be prepared, and when it should be consumed. Jewish kosher laws, Islamic halal practices, and Hindu vegetarianism are all examples of how religion shapes culinary traditions. During religious holidays, special foods are often prepared and shared, reinforcing faith and communal identity. The breaking of the fast during Ramadan with dates and a meal called "iftar" is a powerful symbol of community and spiritual reflection in the Muslim world.

Modern gastronomy continues to reflect and shape cultural trends. The rise of food movements, such as organic farming, farm-to-table dining, and plant-based diets, mirrors broader societal concerns about health, sustainability, and ethical consumption. Chefs and food activists are at the forefront of these movements, using their platforms to advocate for change and to educate the public about the cultural and environmental impact of their food choices. The popularity of food documentaries and cooking shows has also brought greater visibility to these issues, highlighting the connection between what we eat and the world around us.

The digital age has transformed the way we engage with gastronomy and culture. Social media platforms like Instagram and YouTube have made food a global visual language, allowing people to share and discover culinary traditions from around the world. Food bloggers and influencers play a significant role in shaping contemporary food culture, introducing audiences to new ingredients, recipes, and dining experiences. This digital exchange has democratized culinary knowledge, making it accessible to a wider audience and fostering a sense of global culinary community.

Education and gastronomy are closely linked in the transmission of cultural values and practices. Cooking schools, culinary programs, and food literacy initiatives help preserve traditional techniques and inspire new generations of chefs and home cooks. These educational efforts ensure that culinary heritage is not lost and that the cultural significance of food is passed on. They also encourage innovation, as students learn to blend traditional methods with modern techniques, creating new expressions of cultural identity through food.

At its heart, the role of gastronomy in culture is about connection. Food brings people together, whether around a family dinner table, at a festive celebration, or through a shared culinary experience online. It connects us to our past, grounding us in our heritage and traditions, while also linking us to the broader human community through the shared experience of eating. Understanding this role enriches our appreciation of food, transforming it from a mere necessity into a profound expression of who we are and what we value.

Key Elements of a Gastronomic Experience

A gastronomic experience is an immersive journey that engages all the senses, transcending the mere act of eating. It is an art form that combines culinary expertise, creativity, and a deep understanding of the ingredients and their origins. To craft a memorable gastronomic experience, several key elements must harmoniously come together, creating a symphony of flavors, textures, and aromas that delight and surprise.

At the heart of any gastronomic experience is the quality of the ingredients. The foundation of exceptional cuisine lies in the use of fresh, high-quality products. Sourcing ingredients from local farmers, artisanal producers, and sustainable suppliers not only supports local economies but also ensures the freshest and most flavorful components. The taste of a tomato ripened on the vine or a fish caught that morning cannot be replicated by mass-produced alternatives. When chefs prioritize quality, the natural flavors of the ingredients shine, elevating the entire dining experience.

Seasonality is another crucial element in gastronomy. Cooking with seasonal ingredients means utilizing produce at the peak of its flavor and nutritional value. This practice not only results in better-tasting dishes but also aligns with sustainable and ethical food practices. Seasonal cooking encourages creativity as chefs adapt their menus to the changing availability of ingredients, leading to a dynamic and evolving culinary repertoire. For example, a spring menu might feature tender asparagus and fresh peas, while autumn brings hearty squashes and root vegetables to the table.

The art of preparation is where the skill and creativity of the chef come into play. Mastery of culinary techniques, from basic knife skills to advanced cooking methods like sous-vide or molecular gastronomy, is essential. These techniques transform raw ingredients into complex and nuanced dishes, each with its own unique texture and flavor profile. A perfectly seared piece of meat, a delicately poached egg, or a flawlessly executed soufflé all demonstrate the chef's proficiency and attention to detail. The ability to balance flavors, textures, and temperatures is what distinguishes a good dish from an extraordinary one.

Presentation is an often-overlooked yet vital component of the gastronomic experience. The visual appeal of a dish can greatly enhance the overall enjoyment of a meal. Plating techniques, the use of color, and the arrangement of elements on the plate all contribute to the aesthetic experience. Each dish is a canvas, and the chef is the artist, using ingredients to create visually stunning compositions that entice the diner even before the first bite. A beautifully presented dish sets the stage for the sensory journey that follows, making the dining experience more memorable.

Aromas play a significant role in shaping the gastronomic experience. The sense of smell is closely linked to the perception of taste, and the aromas wafting from a dish can evoke powerful memories and emotions. The scent of fresh herbs, the smoky aroma of grilled meats, or the fragrant spices in a curry all contribute to the overall sensory experience. Chefs often use aromatic elements like herbs, spices, and citrus zest to enhance the olfactory appeal of their dishes, creating a multi-sensory experience that begins with the first whiff.

Texture is another key element that adds depth and complexity to a dish. The contrast between crispy and creamy, tender and crunchy, or smooth and chunky can create a more engaging and satisfying dining experience. Achieving the right texture requires precision in cooking techniques, from the perfect al dente pasta to the delicate crunch of a caramelized sugar topping. The interplay of different textures keeps the palate interested and adds layers of enjoyment to each bite.

Context and ambiance also play crucial roles in the gastronomic experience. The setting in which a meal is enjoyed can greatly influence the perception of the food. A beautifully designed dining space, attentive service, and a relaxed atmosphere all contribute to the overall enjoyment of the meal. The ambiance should complement the cuisine, whether it's the cozy charm of a rustic bistro or the sleek elegance of a fine dining restaurant. Attention to detail in the dining environment, from lighting and music to table settings and décor, enhances the sense of occasion and elevates the dining experience.

The narrative behind a dish or a meal can also enrich the gastronomic experience. Storytelling in gastronomy involves sharing the origins of ingredients, the inspiration behind recipes, and the cultural or personal significance of certain dishes. This narrative can create a deeper connection between the diner and the food, transforming the meal into a meaningful experience. For instance, a chef might explain the traditional techniques used to prepare a dish, or how a particular recipe has been passed down through generations. This storytelling adds an emotional dimension to the meal, making it more memorable and engaging.

The element of surprise can transform a good meal into an unforgettable experience. Unexpected flavor combinations, innovative presentations, or theatrical elements like tableside preparations can delight and intrigue diners. The element of surprise keeps the dining experience dynamic and exciting, encouraging diners to explore and appreciate new culinary horizons. This sense of wonder and discovery is a hallmark of truly exceptional gastronomy.

Pairing food with beverages is another aspect that can elevate the gastronomic experience. Thoughtfully selected wine, beer, or cocktail pairings can complement and enhance the flavors of a dish. The right pairing can highlight certain notes in the food, create harmonious contrasts, or cleanse the palate between bites. Sommeliers and beverage experts play a crucial role in curating these pairings, using their knowledge to enhance the overall dining experience. Whether it's the perfect wine to accompany a cheese course or a craft cocktail to complement a dessert, these pairings add another layer of sophistication and enjoyment to the meal.

Finally, the service provided during a meal is integral to the overall experience. Attentive, knowledgeable, and friendly service can make diners feel welcome and valued, enhancing their enjoyment of the meal. Good service involves not only delivering food and drinks efficiently but also anticipating diners' needs and preferences. A well-trained staff can provide insights into the menu, suggest pairings, and accommodate special requests, creating a personalized and seamless dining experience. The interaction between diners and staff can significantly

impact the overall perception of the meal, making
excellent service a key component of a successful
gastronomic experience.

The Future of Gastronomy

The future of gastronomy is a dynamic and evolving
landscape shaped by innovation, sustainability, and
cultural shifts. As we look ahead, several key trends
and developments promise to redefine how we
experience food, from the way it's produced and
prepared to the ways we enjoy it. Understanding
these trends allows us to anticipate and embrace the
changes that will shape the culinary world in the
coming years.

One of the most significant trends in the future of
gastronomy is the emphasis on sustainability. With
growing awareness of environmental issues, there is
an increasing focus on sustainable food practices.
This includes everything from sourcing ingredients
locally to reduce carbon footprints, to adopting
agricultural practices that preserve soil health and
biodiversity. Chefs and restaurateurs are increasingly
committed to reducing food waste, supporting
ethical farming, and offering plant-based menu
options to cater to environmentally conscious diners.
The movement towards sustainable gastronomy not
only helps protect the planet but also encourages

innovation in the kitchen, as chefs experiment with new ingredients and methods.

Technology continues to play a pivotal role in the evolution of gastronomy. Advances in technology are transforming every aspect of the culinary world, from how food is grown to how it is served. Vertical farming, for instance, allows for the cultivation of fresh produce in urban environments, reducing the need for long-distance transportation and ensuring year-round availability. In the kitchen, precision cooking tools like sous-vide machines and smart ovens enable chefs to achieve consistent, high-quality results with greater ease. Furthermore, the rise of food delivery apps and virtual kitchens is changing the traditional restaurant model, making gourmet food more accessible to a broader audience.

The future of gastronomy is also marked by a deepening appreciation for cultural diversity. As globalization continues to break down barriers, there is a growing interest in exploring and celebrating the culinary traditions of different cultures. This trend is leading to the fusion of flavors and techniques, creating exciting new dishes that reflect a blend of influences. Chefs are increasingly drawing inspiration from global cuisines, incorporating exotic spices, unique cooking methods, and traditional recipes into their menus. This cultural exchange enriches the culinary landscape, offering diners a taste of the world without leaving their hometown.

Health and wellness are becoming central to the future of gastronomy. With a heightened awareness of the link between diet and health, there is a growing demand for nutritious, wholesome foods. Chefs are responding by creating menus that emphasize fresh, unprocessed ingredients, and balance flavor with nutritional value. Trends like plant-based diets, fermented foods, and functional ingredients such as adaptogens and probiotics are gaining popularity. The focus on health extends beyond individual dishes to entire dining experiences, with restaurants offering wellness-focused menus and even integrating fitness and mindfulness into their offerings.

The concept of experiential dining is evolving, driven by a desire for more immersive and memorable culinary experiences. This goes beyond the food itself to encompass the entire dining environment and the emotional journey of the diner. Restaurants are experimenting with multisensory elements, such as incorporating music, lighting, and even scent to enhance the dining experience. Pop-up restaurants, themed dining events, and chef's table experiences offer unique and intimate settings where diners can interact with chefs and gain insight into the creative process. This trend towards experiential dining reflects a broader shift towards valuing experiences over material goods.

Another exciting development in the future of gastronomy is the rise of personalized dining experiences. Advances in data analytics and artificial intelligence are enabling restaurants to offer highly customized meals based on individual preferences and dietary needs. From personalized menus that cater to specific allergies and intolerances to dishes tailored to a diner's flavor profile, the possibilities for customization are expanding. This level of personalization enhances the dining experience, making it more enjoyable and satisfying for each guest.

Innovation in food science is opening up new frontiers in gastronomy. Molecular gastronomy, which explores the physical and chemical transformations of ingredients during cooking, has already revolutionized the culinary world with techniques like spherification and foams. Looking ahead, we can expect even more groundbreaking developments as scientists and chefs collaborate to push the boundaries of what is possible. From 3D-printed food to lab-grown meat, these innovations have the potential to change not only what we eat but also how we think about food production and consumption.

The role of storytelling in gastronomy is becoming increasingly important. Diners are not just interested in what they are eating, but also in the stories behind the food. This includes the origins of ingredients, the journey of the chef, and the cultural significance of the dishes. Storytelling adds depth and meaning to the dining experience, creating a connection between the diner and the food. Chefs and restaurateurs are finding creative ways to share these stories, whether through menu descriptions, personal interactions, or multimedia presentations. This emphasis on storytelling enriches the dining experience, making it more engaging and memorable.

Looking to the future, the concept of food sovereignty is gaining traction. Food sovereignty emphasizes the right of people to define their own food systems, prioritizing local, sustainable practices over global, industrial ones. This movement is driven by a desire to reclaim control over food production and promote food justice, ensuring that all communities have access to healthy, culturally appropriate food. By supporting local farmers, preserving traditional foodways, and advocating for equitable food policies, the food sovereignty movement aligns with broader efforts to create a more just and sustainable food system.

The future of gastronomy is also shaped by the increasing importance of community and social connection. Food has always been a means of bringing people together, and this aspect is becoming even more significant in our fast-paced, digital world. Community-focused dining experiences, such as communal tables, food festivals, and cooking classes, foster a sense of connection and shared experience. Restaurants and chefs are also playing a role in addressing social issues, from supporting local food banks to creating inclusive spaces that welcome diverse communities. This focus on community reflects a broader recognition of the social and cultural dimensions of food.

As we look ahead, it is clear that the future of gastronomy will be defined by a blend of tradition and innovation. Chefs and food professionals will continue to honor the rich heritage of culinary traditions while embracing new technologies and ideas. Sustainability, health, and cultural diversity will remain central themes, driving the evolution of the culinary landscape. By staying attuned to these trends and developments, we can not only anticipate the future of gastronomy but also actively shape it, creating a more delicious, sustainable, and inclusive world of food.

Chapter 2

European Culinary Traditions

French Cuisine: The Art of Haute Cuisine

French cuisine, often referred to as the pinnacle of culinary art, has a storied history and a profound influence on global gastronomy. Its evolution from royal court feasts to modern haute cuisine is a testament to its enduring allure and complexity. At its heart, French cuisine is about precision, technique, and a deep respect for ingredients. This chapter delves into the nuances of haute cuisine, exploring its origins, key techniques, and how aspiring chefs can master this sophisticated culinary style.

The roots of haute cuisine can be traced back to the 17th century, during the reign of Louis XIV. The King's lavish banquets at the Palace of Versailles set the stage for what would become a hallmark of French culture. These grand feasts required meticulous planning and execution, with dishes that not only tantalized the taste buds but also dazzled the eyes. This period saw the emergence of cooks like François Pierre La Varenne, who documented the principles of French cooking in his seminal work, "Le Cuisinier François." La Varenne's techniques and recipes laid the groundwork for modern French cuisine, emphasizing the importance of sauces, stocks, and precise cooking methods.

One of the defining characteristics of French haute cuisine is its reliance on classic techniques. Mastering these techniques is essential for any chef aspiring to excel in this culinary tradition. For instance, the preparation of a perfect sauce is a cornerstone of French cooking. Sauces in French cuisine are not merely accompaniments; they are integral components that enhance the flavors of the main ingredients. The five "mother sauces" – Béchamel, Velouté, Espagnole, Sauce Tomat, and Hollandaise – form the foundation, from which countless variations can be crafted. Each requires a specific method and a keen eye for detail to achieve the desired consistency and flavor balance.

Another key technique is the art of braising. This method involves slow-cooking meat or vegetables in a covered pot with a small amount of liquid. The goal is to break down tough fibers, resulting in tender and flavorful dishes. Classic examples include Coq au Vin and Boeuf Bourguignon, where the meat is braised in wine, infusing it with rich, deep flavors. Understanding the principles of braising – from selecting the right cut of meat to controlling the cooking temperature – is crucial for creating authentic French dishes.

Presentation, too, plays a vital role in haute cuisine. French chefs are renowned for their meticulous plating, where every element on the plate serves a purpose and contributes to an overall aesthetic. The arrangement of food is considered an art form, with a focus on harmony, color, and texture. A beautifully presented dish not only pleases the eye but also sets the stage for an unforgettable dining experience. Aspiring chefs must develop a keen sense of visual composition, learning how to balance elements and create visually appealing plates that enhance the dining experience.

The concept of terroir is deeply embedded in French cuisine. Terroir refers to the unique characteristics imparted by a specific region's climate, soil, and geography to the food produced there. French chefs emphasize the use of local and seasonal ingredients, believing that these elements contribute to the authenticity and quality of their dishes. This respect for terroir is evident in the regional diversity of French cuisine, from the buttery pastries of Brittany to the hearty stews of Provence. To truly embrace French haute cuisine, one must understand and appreciate the importance of using the freshest, highest-quality ingredients available.

The role of the chef in French cuisine is both demanding and revered. A chef must possess not only technical skills but also creativity, discipline, and a deep understanding of the culinary arts. The journey to becoming a master chef typically begins with rigorous training, often in the form of apprenticeships under established chefs. This hands-on experience is invaluable, providing aspiring chefs with the opportunity to learn the intricacies of French cooking and develop their own style. Formal education at prestigious culinary schools, such as Le Cordon Bleu in Paris, further hones their skills and knowledge, preparing them for the challenges of the culinary world.

French cuisine also places a strong emphasis on the dining experience as a whole. Dining in France is often a leisurely affair, with multiple courses and a focus on savoring each bite. A typical French meal might begin with an amuse-bouche, a small, flavorful bite designed to whet the appetite. This is followed by a series of carefully curated courses, each building on the flavors of the previous one. The meal often concludes with a selection of cheeses and a delicate dessert, leaving the diner with a sense of satisfaction and delight. Understanding the rhythm and flow of a traditional French meal is essential for creating an authentic dining experience.

Innovation within the framework of tradition is another hallmark of haute cuisine. While French chefs respect the classical techniques and flavors, they are also known for their willingness to experiment and push boundaries. This spirit of innovation has led to the development of nouvelle cuisine in the 1960s, which emphasized lighter, more delicate dishes and a greater focus on presentation. Today, modern French chefs continue to blend tradition with contemporary techniques, creating dishes that honor the past while embracing the future. This balance of old and new is what keeps French cuisine vibrant and relevant in the ever-evolving culinary landscape.

For beginners looking to master the art of French haute cuisine, starting with the basics is crucial. Learning to make a perfect stock, mastering the mother sauces, and practicing classic techniques like braising and roasting are foundational skills. Building a repertoire of traditional dishes, such as Ratatouille, Quiche Lorraine, and Tarte Tatin, provides a solid grounding in French culinary principles. As confidence and skills grow, aspiring chefs can begin to experiment with more complex recipes and techniques, always striving for precision and excellence.

Understanding the importance of seasonality and sourcing quality ingredients cannot be overstated.

Visiting local markets, developing relationships with trusted suppliers, and learning about the produce of different regions are all part of the journey. This knowledge not only enhances the flavor and authenticity of the dishes but also connects the chef to the broader food culture and traditions of France.

Italian Cuisine: Passion and Tradition

Italian cuisine, a symphony of flavors and traditions, captivates the heart and soul of anyone who experiences it. It is a cuisine that speaks of family, passion, and an unwavering respect for ingredients. From the rolling hills of Tuscany to the vibrant streets of Naples, the diversity of Italian food reflects the rich tapestry of its regions. This chapter delves into the essence of Italian cuisine, exploring its historical roots, fundamental techniques, and the timeless recipes that continue to define it.

Italy's culinary history is deeply intertwined with its cultural evolution. The ancient Romans were among the first to document their culinary practices, laying the groundwork for many techniques and recipes that endure today. Roman feasts were elaborate affairs, often featuring a variety of meats, fish, and vegetables, seasoned with herbs and spices that showcased their sophisticated palate. The fall of the

Roman Empire led to the rise of regional cuisines, each developing its unique character based on local ingredients and traditions.

Central to Italian cooking is the concept of *la cucina povera*, or "the cuisine of the poor." This approach emphasizes simplicity and resourcefulness, making the most of available ingredients. It is this philosophy that birthed many beloved Italian dishes. For instance, *panzanella*, a bread salad from Tuscany, transforms stale bread into a flavorful dish with the addition of tomatoes, onions, and basil. Similarly, *ribollita*, a hearty vegetable soup, exemplifies the ingenuity of Italian home cooks who repurpose leftovers into something delectable.

One cannot discuss Italian cuisine without mentioning pasta, a staple that has become synonymous with the country's culinary identity. The art of pasta-making varies significantly across regions, each boasting its own shapes and sauces. In the north, rich, creamy sauces like *alfredo* and *carbonara* reign supreme, while the south favors vibrant, tomato-based sauces. Mastering the perfect pasta dish requires understanding the balance of flavors and textures. Fresh pasta, made from simple ingredients like flour and eggs, embodies the essence of Italian cooking — humble yet exquisite. Learning to make pasta from scratch is an essential skill for any aspiring chef, allowing for endless possibilities and personal touches.

Pizza, another iconic Italian creation, has a history as rich as its flavor. Originating in Naples, the pizza we know today evolved from humble flatbreads topped with ingredients accessible to the poor. The classic Margherita pizza, with its simple combination of tomatoes, mozzarella, and basil, symbolizes the colors of the Italian flag and the beauty of simplicity. Achieving the perfect pizza involves mastering dough techniques, understanding fermentation, and balancing toppings to create a harmonious bite.

Italian cuisine's reverence for ingredients extends to its use of seasonal produce. The Mediterranean climate blesses Italy with an abundance of fresh fruits, vegetables, and herbs, which are integral to its dishes. The concept of *stagionalità*, or seasonality, is deeply ingrained in Italian cooking. Chefs and home cooks alike prioritize using ingredients at their peak, ensuring maximum flavor and nutritional value. Seasonal cooking not only enhances the taste of dishes but also fosters a connection to the land and its cycles.

The Italian meal structure is a reflection of the country's social fabric. Meals are often leisurely and communal, with multiple courses that encourage savoring each moment. A traditional Italian meal begins with *antipasti*, a selection of appetizers that

might include cured meats, cheeses, and marinated vegetables. This is followed by *primo*, the first course, typically consisting of pasta, risotto, or soup.
The *secondo*, or main course, features meat or fish, accompanied by a side dish known as *contorno*. The meal concludes with *dolce*, a dessert that ranges from light, refreshing sorbets to decadent cakes and pastries. Understanding this structure helps aspiring chefs appreciate the rhythm and flow of Italian dining, creating experiences that are both satisfying and memorable.

One of the most beautiful aspects of Italian cuisine is its emphasis on family and tradition. Recipes are often passed down through generations, each adding their unique touch while preserving the essence of the dish. This culinary heritage is celebrated in Italian households, where cooking is a communal activity, and meals are a time to gather and connect. The kitchen serves as the heart of the home, a place where stories are shared, and bonds are strengthened over pots of simmering sauce.

Wine, too, plays an integral role in Italian cuisine. Italy's diverse climate and geography produce a wide range of wines, each complementing different dishes. From the robust reds of Tuscany to the crisp whites of Veneto, understanding the basics of Italian wine enhances the dining experience. Pairing wine with food is an art, requiring knowledge of flavor profiles and regional characteristics. A well-chosen wine can elevate a meal, bringing out the nuances of the food and creating a harmonious balance.

For beginners eager to dive into Italian cuisine, starting with foundational dishes is essential. Learning to make a basic tomato sauce, mastering the art of risotto, and perfecting the technique of making pizza dough are all crucial skills. These dishes form the backbone of Italian cooking and provide a solid foundation upon which more complex recipes can be built. Experimentation is encouraged, but always with a respect for tradition and a focus on quality ingredients.

Italian desserts offer a delightful end to any meal. Classics like *tiramisu*, *cannoli*, and *panna cotta* showcase the country's love for sweets. These desserts often feature simple ingredients like mascarpone, ricotta, and fresh fruits, allowing the flavors to shine. Mastering these recipes requires precision and patience, but the reward is well worth the effort. Serving a homemade Italian dessert can be a point of pride and a testament to one's culinary skills.

The journey into Italian cuisine is one of discovery and joy. It is about more than just cooking; it is about embracing a way of life that values good food, family, and tradition. Each dish tells a story, each meal is a celebration. By immersing oneself in the techniques and principles of Italian cooking, one gains not only culinary skills but also a deeper appreciation for the culture and heritage that underpin this beloved cuisine.

Spanish Tapas: Small Plates, Big Flavors

Spanish tapas, the quintessential embodiment of Spain's vibrant culinary culture, offer a unique and engaging way to experience the country's diverse flavors. These small plates, often enjoyed with a glass of wine or beer, are more than just appetizers; they represent a social dining experience that brings people together. Originating in Andalusia, tapas have evolved into a nationwide phenomenon, each region contributing its own specialties and interpretations. This chapter explores the rich history, essential techniques, and classic recipes that make Spanish tapas a beloved tradition.

The origin of tapas is shrouded in delightful legends. One popular story suggests that King Alfonso X of Castile decreed that taverns should serve food with wine to prevent overindulgence. Another tale recounts how bartenders used slices of bread or ham to cover glasses of wine, protecting them from flies. Regardless of their beginnings, tapas have become an integral part of Spanish life, reflecting the country's convivial spirit and love for flavorful, shared meals.

At the heart of tapas culture is the idea of variety. A typical tapas spread includes an array of dishes, each offering a distinct taste and texture. This diversity allows diners to sample a wide range of flavors in one sitting, from the salty punch of olives to the creamy richness of *croquetas*. For beginners, mastering a few key recipes provides a solid foundation for building a tapas repertoire.

A cornerstone of any tapas menu is the *tortilla española*, a simple yet delicious potato omelet. Made with just a few ingredients—potatoes, onions, eggs, and olive oil—this dish exemplifies the Spanish knack for transforming humble ingredients into something extraordinary. The key to a perfect tortilla lies in slow-cooking the potatoes and onions until they are tender and caramelized, then gently folding them into beaten eggs and cooking the mixture until it sets. Served warm or at room temperature, tortilla española is a versatile dish that can be enjoyed at any time of day.

Another essential tapa is *patatas bravas*, crispy fried potatoes topped with a spicy tomato sauce and a garlicky aioli. This dish showcases the bold flavors that characterize Spanish cuisine. The potatoes are typically parboiled before frying to achieve a crispy exterior and a fluffy interior. The bravas sauce, made from tomatoes, paprika, and chili peppers, adds a fiery kick, while the aioli provides a creamy, garlicky contrast. Together, these elements create a harmonious and satisfying bite.

Seafood plays a prominent role in tapas, reflecting Spain's extensive coastline and rich maritime heritage. *Gambas al ajillo*, or garlic shrimp, is a classic seafood tapa that highlights the simplicity and freshness of Spanish cooking. Shrimp are sautéed in olive oil with generous amounts of garlic and a touch of chili, creating a dish that is both fragrant and flavorful. The key to this dish is not overcooking the shrimp, ensuring they remain tender and juicy. Served with crusty bread to soak up the garlicky oil, gambas al ajillo is a crowd-pleaser that never fails to impress.

No tapas spread would be complete without *jamón ibérico*, thinly sliced cured ham from the Iberian Peninsula. This delicacy, known for its rich, nutty flavor and melt-in-your-mouth texture, is a testament to Spain's long-standing tradition of ham curing. Produced from Iberian pigs that roam freely and feed on acorns, jamón ibérico undergoes a meticulous curing process that can last for years. The result is a product of unparalleled quality, often enjoyed on its own or with a simple accompaniment of bread and tomatoes.

Cheese lovers will delight in *queso manchego*, a sheep's milk cheese from the La Mancha region. Aged for varying lengths of time, Manchego offers a range of flavors from mild and creamy to sharp and nutty. It pairs beautifully with quince paste, known as *membrillo*, creating a delightful contrast of sweet and savory. Incorporating cheese into a tapas menu adds another layer of complexity and satisfaction.

Tapas also embrace the bounty of Spain's vegetable gardens. *Pimientos de padrón*, small green peppers fried until blistered and sprinkled with sea salt, are a seasonal favorite. Most are mild, but occasionally a spicy one sneaks in, adding an element of surprise to the dish. This simple preparation allows the natural flavor of the peppers to shine, making them a perfect accompaniment to more robust dishes.

For those with a sweet tooth, *churros con chocolate* offers a delightful end to a tapas meal. These deep-fried dough sticks, dusted with sugar and served with a thick, rich chocolate sauce, are a popular treat in Spain. The contrast between the crispy exterior and the soft, doughy interior, combined with the indulgent chocolate, creates a dessert that is both comforting and decadent. Making churros at home requires a bit of practice, but the result is well worth the effort, providing a sweet conclusion to a savory feast.

The social aspect of tapas cannot be overstated. In Spain, dining is a communal activity, and tapas are designed to be shared. This encourages a relaxed, convivial atmosphere where conversation flows as freely as the wine. Hosting a tapas party at home can recreate this experience, bringing friends and family together to enjoy a variety of dishes. Preparing a selection of tapas allows for creativity and experimentation, giving cooks the opportunity to showcase their skills and introduce guests to new flavors.

Pairing wine with tapas enhances the dining experience, each sip complementing and elevating the flavors of the food. Spain boasts a rich wine heritage, with regions like Rioja and Ribera del Duero producing some of the world's finest wines. A crisp white *Albariño* pairs beautifully with seafood tapas, while a robust red *Tempranillo* complements heartier dishes like tortilla española and patatas bravas. Understanding basic wine pairings can enhance the enjoyment of tapas, creating a harmonious balance between food and drink.

For beginners, starting with a few simple tapas recipes provides a foundation upon which to build. Experimenting with different ingredients and techniques allows for personalization and creativity. The key to successful tapas lies in the quality of the ingredients and the care taken in their preparation.

Fresh, high-quality produce, meats, and seafood are essential, as is the use of good olive oil and spices.

British Classics: From Pies to Puddings

British cuisine, often unfairly maligned for its simplicity, boasts a rich tapestry of flavors and traditions. From hearty pies to decadent puddings, the country's culinary classics reflect its agricultural bounty and historical influences. These dishes, steeped in tradition and often passed down through generations, offer a comforting taste of home for many. Understanding the techniques and ingredients that make these classics so beloved is key to mastering British cooking.

Pies, in particular, hold a special place in British hearts. They are a symbol of comfort and nourishment, perfect for the country's chilly climate. The most iconic of these is the steak and ale pie. This robust dish combines tender chunks of beef with rich, malty ale, all encased in a flaky pastry. The secret to a great steak and ale pie lies in the slow cooking of the beef, allowing it to become melt-in-your-mouth tender and infusing the gravy with deep, savory flavors. The pastry should be golden and crisp, providing a perfect contrast to the hearty filling.

Another beloved pie is the Cornish pasty. This portable, crescent-shaped pie originated in Cornwall and was traditionally a miner's lunch. Filled with a mixture of beef, potatoes, swede (or rutabaga), and onions, the Cornish pasty is both nutritious and satisfying. The pastry, made with lard and flour, is sturdy enough to hold up to a day in a miner's pocket, yet tender and flavorful. Crimping the edges of the pasty not only seals in the filling but also provides a signature look that sets it apart from other pies.

Puddings, both savory and sweet, are another cornerstone of British cuisine. The term "pudding" in Britain encompasses a wide range of dishes, from steamed suet puddings to creamy desserts. One of the most iconic savory puddings is Yorkshire pudding, traditionally served with roast beef. This light and airy batter pudding, made from eggs, flour, and milk, rises dramatically in the oven, creating a crispy exterior and a soft, doughy interior. The key to a perfect Yorkshire pudding is a hot oven and preheating the fat in the baking tin, which helps the batter rise quickly and evenly.

On the sweet side, the British excel in creating comforting, indulgent desserts. Sticky toffee pudding, a moist sponge cake made with dates and drenched in a rich toffee sauce, is a prime example. This dessert, often served with a dollop of clotted cream or a scoop of vanilla ice cream, is a beloved treat that combines the sweetness of dates with the buttery, caramel notes of the toffee sauce. The cake itself should be soft and tender, absorbing the sauce without becoming soggy.

Another classic is the treacle tart, a sweet pastry case filled with a mixture of golden syrup, breadcrumbs, and lemon juice. This dessert, with its sticky, citrusy filling and crisp pastry, is a nostalgic favorite for many Britons. The breadcrumbs give the tart a unique texture, while the lemon juice cuts through the sweetness of the syrup, creating a balanced and delightful treat. Serving treacle tart with a dollop of clotted cream or a splash of custard enhances its rich flavors.

British cuisine also includes a variety of regional specialties, each with its own unique charm. From the Scottish haggis, a savory pudding made from sheep's offal, oatmeal, and spices, to the Welsh rarebit, a rich cheese sauce served on toast, these dishes reflect the diverse culinary heritage of the United Kingdom. Haggis, often served with "neeps and tatties" (turnips and potatoes), is a dish that celebrates the resourcefulness and ingenuity of Scottish cooks. Despite its humble ingredients, haggis is rich and flavorful, with a distinct spiciness that comes from black pepper and other seasonings.

Welsh rarebit, on the other hand, is a simple yet luxurious dish that elevates humble ingredients. The cheese sauce, made with sharp cheddar, mustard, and ale or milk, is poured over thick slices of toasted bread and grilled until bubbly and golden. This dish, often enjoyed as a snack or light meal, showcases the rich dairy heritage of Wales and the British love for cheese.

No exploration of British classics would be complete without mentioning the full English breakfast. This hearty meal, traditionally eaten to start the day, includes a variety of components: eggs, bacon, sausages, black pudding, baked beans, grilled tomatoes, and mushrooms. Each element is cooked separately, allowing for individual perfection, and then assembled on a plate for a feast that satisfies the heartiest of appetites. The black pudding, a type of blood sausage, adds a rich, earthy flavor to the plate, while the baked beans provide a touch of sweetness. The grilled tomatoes and mushrooms add freshness and balance, making the full English breakfast a well-rounded and satisfying meal.

For those who prefer a lighter start to the day, British cuisine offers the delightfully simple crumpet. These small, round griddle cakes, with their characteristic holes, are perfect for soaking up butter and jam. Made from a yeast-risen batter, crumpets are cooked on a hot griddle until their tops are full of tiny bubbles and their bottoms are golden brown. The texture of a crumpet should be light and spongy, providing a perfect base for a generous spread of butter and a dollop of jam or honey.

Afternoon tea, a quintessentially British tradition, also showcases an array of classic treats. Delicate finger sandwiches, scones with clotted cream and jam, and an assortment of pastries and cakes are served alongside pots of tea. Scones, in particular, are a highlight of this ritual. These crumbly, slightly sweet biscuits are best enjoyed fresh from the oven, split open, and slathered with thick clotted cream and a spoonful of jam. The combination of the warm, tender scone with the cool, creamy clotted cream and the fruity jam is nothing short of sublime.

The British love for puddings extends to the festive season, with Christmas pudding being a standout. This dense, steamed dessert, made with dried fruits, spices, and suet, is often prepared weeks in advance to allow the flavors to mature. Traditionally, a small coin is hidden inside the pudding, bringing good luck to the person who finds it. Served with a rich brandy butter or a creamy custard, Christmas pudding is a fittingly indulgent end to the holiday meal.

Mastering British classics involves understanding the balance of flavors and textures that define these dishes. The use of high-quality ingredients, attention to detail in preparation, and a respect for tradition are all essential. While some recipes may seem daunting at first, the rewards are well worth the effort. These dishes, with their comforting familiarity and robust flavors, offer a taste of Britain's culinary heritage that is both timeless and universally appealing.

Scandinavian Simplicity: Fresh and Natural

Scandinavian cuisine, celebrated for its minimalism and reliance on fresh, natural ingredients, offers a refreshing contrast to more elaborate culinary traditions. The simplicity of these dishes belies their depth of flavor and nutritional value. Rooted in the region's harsh climate and limited growing season, Scandinavian cuisine has evolved to make the most of what nature provides, emphasizing preservation techniques and seasonal produce. Understanding this approach is key to mastering the art of Scandinavian cooking.

Central to Scandinavian simplicity is the concept of "lagom," a Swedish term meaning "just the right amount." This philosophy is evident in the balanced flavors and restrained use of ingredients. Rather than masking the natural taste of food with heavy sauces or excessive seasoning, Scandinavian cooks focus on enhancing the inherent qualities of each ingredient. This results in dishes that are clean, bright, and true to their origins.

One of the most iconic elements of Scandinavian cuisine is the smörgåsbord, a buffet-style meal featuring a variety of cold and hot dishes. This spread typically includes cured fish, such as gravlax and pickled herring, alongside an array of breads, cheeses, and meats. Gravlax, a cured salmon dish, is a prime example of the region's culinary ingenuity. The salmon is cured with a mixture of salt, sugar, and dill, resulting in a tender, flavorful fish that is both simple and elegant. The process of curing not only preserves the fish but also concentrates its flavors, making it a delicacy that is perfect for any occasion.

Pickled herring, another staple of the smörgåsbord, showcases the Scandinavian mastery of preservation techniques. Herring, a common fish in the region's cold waters, is pickled in a mixture of vinegar, sugar, and spices. This method extends the fish's shelf life while imparting a tangy, slightly sweet flavor that pairs beautifully with dense rye bread and boiled potatoes. The contrast between the sharpness of the vinegar and the richness of the fish creates a harmonious balance that is quintessentially Scandinavian.

Bread plays a significant role in Scandinavian cuisine, with dark, dense varieties like rye and pumpernickel being particularly popular. These breads, often made with whole grains and seeds, provide a hearty base for open-faced sandwiches, known as smørrebrød in Denmark. These sandwiches are a canvas for a variety of toppings, from cured meats and cheeses to fresh vegetables and spreads. The beauty of smørrebrød lies in its simplicity; each ingredient is allowed to shine, creating a meal that is both satisfying and visually appealing.

Cheese is another important component of the Scandinavian diet, with varieties like Swedish Västerbotten, Danish Havarti, and Norwegian Gjetost offering a range of flavors and textures. Västerbotten, a hard cheese with a sharp, nutty taste, is often grated over dishes or enjoyed on its own. Havarti, a semi-soft cheese with a buttery flavor, melts beautifully, making it ideal for sandwiches and baking. Gjetost, a caramel-colored cheese made from goat's milk, has a unique sweet and tangy flavor that pairs well with crispbread and fruit.

Seasonality is a cornerstone of Scandinavian cooking, with dishes often reflecting the availability of local produce. In the summer months, the region's long daylight hours result in an abundance of fresh berries, vegetables, and herbs. Strawberries, raspberries, and blueberries are particularly prized, often featured in desserts like rødgrød, a Danish red berry pudding. This dish, made by simmering berries with sugar and thickening the mixture with potato starch, is served chilled with a splash of cream, offering a refreshing end to a summer meal.

Root vegetables, such as potatoes, carrots, and beets, are staples of the Scandinavian winter diet. These hardy crops store well, providing essential nutrients during the cold months. Potatoes, in particular, are incredibly versatile and feature prominently in many traditional dishes. Janssons frestelse, a Swedish potato casserole, combines thinly sliced potatoes with onions, anchovies, and cream, resulting in a rich, savory dish that is both comforting and satisfying. The anchovies add a depth of flavor that complements the sweetness of the onions and the creaminess of the potatoes.

Preservation techniques, such as smoking, pickling, and fermenting, are integral to Scandinavian cuisine. These methods not only extend the shelf life of food but also enhance its flavor. Smoked salmon, or røkt laks, is a delicacy enjoyed throughout the region. The salmon is cured with salt and then cold-smoked, imparting a delicate smoky flavor while retaining the fish's tender texture. This technique, developed out of necessity, has become a hallmark of Scandinavian culinary tradition.

Fermented foods, like sauerkraut and pickles, are also common in Scandinavian diets. Fermentation, a natural preservation method, creates beneficial probiotics that promote gut health. Surkål, or Norwegian sauerkraut, is made by fermenting cabbage with salt and caraway seeds, resulting in a tangy, crunchy side dish that pairs well with sausages and meats. The process of fermentation not only preserves the cabbage but also enhances its nutritional value, making it a staple in Scandinavian homes.

Dairy products, such as yogurt and buttermilk, are frequently used in Scandinavian cooking. Filmjölk, a Swedish fermented milk, is similar to yogurt but with a thinner consistency. It is often enjoyed for breakfast with muesli or used in baking to add moisture and tanginess to cakes and breads. Buttermilk, a byproduct of butter-making, is another versatile ingredient, commonly used in marinades, dressings, and baked goods.

Herbs and spices play a subtle yet important role in Scandinavian cuisine. Dill, parsley, and chives are used to add freshness and brightness to dishes. Dill, in particular, is a favorite, often paired with fish and potatoes. Its delicate flavor enhances without overpowering, embodying the Scandinavian penchant for simplicity. Cardamom and cinnamon are popular in baking, lending warmth and complexity to pastries and breads. Cardamom buns, or kardemummabullar, are a beloved Swedish treat, featuring a sweet, spiced dough twisted into intricate shapes and sprinkled with sugar.

Scandinavian desserts, while not overly sweet, offer a delightful end to a meal. Kanelbullar, or Swedish cinnamon buns, are a staple in Scandinavian bakeries. These soft, fragrant rolls are made with a yeasted dough enriched with butter and flavored with cinnamon. They are typically enjoyed with a cup of coffee, embodying the Swedish tradition of "fika," a coffee break that is as much about socializing as it is about the food.

Another classic dessert is the Norwegian kransekake, a towering ring cake made from almond flour, sugar, and egg whites. This festive cake, often decorated with icing and flags, is a staple at weddings and celebrations. Its chewy texture and rich almond flavor make it a memorable treat that is both simple and elegant.

Chapter 3

Asian Culinary Delights

Japanese Precision: Sushi and Beyond

Japanese cuisine, renowned for its precision and artistry, extends far beyond the delicate slices of fish and perfectly seasoned rice that define sushi. This culinary tradition is deeply rooted in a history of meticulous preparation and a profound respect for nature's bounty. Each dish, no matter how simple, is crafted with an attention to detail that borders on the obsessive, ensuring not only visual appeal but also a harmonious balance of flavors and textures.

The heart of Japanese cooking lies in the concept of umami, often referred to as the "fifth taste." Discovered over a century ago, umami is a savory flavor that enhances the depth and richness of food. It can be found in ingredients like soy sauce, miso, seaweed, and fermented fish. Mastering umami is essential for any cook aspiring to replicate the nuanced taste profiles of Japanese dishes.

Sushi, perhaps the most famous Japanese food, exemplifies the precision and simplicity of this culinary tradition. At its core, sushi consists of vinegared rice paired with various toppings, the most popular being raw fish. The key to exceptional sushi lies in the quality and freshness of the ingredients. Fish must be impeccably fresh, often sourced directly from the market and prepared within hours. The rice, seasoned with a delicate balance of vinegar, sugar, and salt, should be slightly warm and sticky enough to hold together without being mushy.

Nigiri sushi, a hand-pressed mound of rice topped with a slice of fish, showcases the importance of technique. The rice must be shaped with a gentle yet firm touch, ensuring it holds its form while remaining light and airy. The fish, sliced with razor-sharp knives, should be cut at an angle to maximize surface area and enhance the texture. A small dab of wasabi between the rice and fish adds a subtle heat that complements the natural sweetness of the seafood.

Maki rolls, another popular form of sushi, involve rolling rice and fillings in a sheet of nori (seaweed). The fillings can range from simple cucumber or avocado to more complex combinations like spicy tuna or tempura shrimp. The roll is then sliced into bite-sized pieces, each revealing a cross-section of the colorful ingredients. Precision is crucial here, as uneven rolling or slicing can result in a messy presentation and uneven distribution of flavors.

Sashimi, the purest expression of raw fish, strips away the rice to focus solely on the seafood. Served with minimal garnish, often just a bit of grated daikon and a shiso leaf, sashimi highlights the natural qualities of the fish. The slices should be uniform in thickness and arranged artfully on the plate, inviting the diner to appreciate the beauty of the ingredients.

Beyond sushi, Japanese cuisine offers a wealth of dishes that embody the same principles of precision and simplicity. Tempura, a method of deep-frying seafood and vegetables in a light, airy batter, demands careful control of temperature and timing. The batter, made from cold water, flour, and sometimes egg, should be mixed just enough to combine, leaving a few lumps to create a crisp texture. The oil must be kept at a consistent temperature, usually around 350°F (175°C), to ensure the perfect golden-brown crust without overcooking the delicate ingredients.

Ramen, a hearty noodle soup, has gained international popularity for its complex broth and customizable toppings. The broth, which can be based on pork, chicken, or miso, requires hours of simmering to develop its rich, umami flavor. The noodles, whether thick and curly or thin and straight, should be cooked to a firm, chewy texture. Toppings like sliced pork, soft-boiled eggs, and scallions add layers of flavor and texture, making each bowl a unique culinary experience.

Another staple of Japanese dining is the bento box, a compartmentalized meal that offers a variety of flavors and textures in a single serving. A typical bento might include rice, grilled fish or meat, pickled vegetables, and a small dessert. The arrangement of the components is as important as the ingredients themselves, with each item placed to create a visually appealing and balanced meal. This attention to detail ensures that every bite is a harmonious blend of tastes and textures.

The practice of kaiseki, a traditional multi-course meal, elevates Japanese cuisine to an art form. Each course is meticulously prepared and presented, often featuring seasonal ingredients that reflect the natural rhythms of the year. The meal begins with a light appetizer, followed by a series of dishes that might include sashimi, grilled fish, simmered vegetables, and a clear soup. The courses are designed to progress in flavor and complexity, culminating in a dessert that provides a sweet, satisfying conclusion.

Integral to Japanese cooking is the use of dashi, a simple broth made from kombu (seaweed) and katsuobushi (dried bonito flakes). Dashi forms the foundation of many soups, sauces, and stews, imparting a subtle umami flavor that enhances the other ingredients. Making dashi is a lesson in simplicity and precision: the kombu is soaked in water to extract its flavor, then gently heated before the katsuobushi is added. Once the flakes sink to the bottom, the broth is strained, resulting in a clear, flavorful liquid that serves as the backbone of many Japanese dishes.

The art of Japanese pickling, known as tsukemono, also deserves mention for its role in balancing and complementing meals. Vegetables like radishes, cucumbers, and plums are preserved in a variety of ways, from simple salt brines to more complex mixtures of vinegar, sugar, and spices. These pickles add a crunchy, tangy contrast to the often subtle flavors of other dishes, providing a refreshing palate cleanser.

Japanese desserts, while not as widely known as their Western counterparts, offer a delightful end to a meal. Mochi, a chewy rice cake, can be filled with sweet red bean paste or flavored with matcha (green tea) powder. Dorayaki, a type of pancake sandwich filled with red bean paste, combines a soft, fluffy exterior with a sweet, smooth filling. These treats, though simple, require precise techniques to achieve the correct texture and flavor balance.

Tea, an essential part of Japanese culture, also reflects the precision and mindfulness inherent in the cuisine. The traditional tea ceremony, or chanoyu, is a ritualized preparation of matcha, a powdered green tea. Every movement, from whisking the tea to presenting the cup, is performed with deliberate grace and attention to detail. This ceremony embodies the Japanese values of harmony, respect, and tranquility.

Chinese Regional Specialties

China's vast and varied landscape is mirrored in its culinary diversity, with each region boasting its own unique flavors, ingredients, and cooking techniques. From the fiery spices of Sichuan to the delicate dim sum of Guangdong, Chinese regional specialties offer a rich tapestry of tastes that reflect the cultural and geographical differences within the country. This chapter delves into some of the most iconic regional dishes and the culinary traditions that have shaped them, providing a window into the soul of Chinese cuisine.

Starting in the north, Beijing is not only the political capital of China but also a culinary hub known for its hearty and flavorful dishes. The most famous of these is Peking Duck, a dish that dates back to the imperial kitchens of the Ming Dynasty. The preparation of Peking Duck is an art form in itself, involving air-drying the duck, glazing it with a maltose syrup, and then roasting it to perfection. The result is a bird with crispy, golden skin and tender, succulent meat. Traditionally, Peking Duck is served with thin pancakes, hoisin sauce, and julienned scallions, allowing diners to create their own savory wraps.

Traveling south to the province of Sichuan, one encounters a cuisine renowned for its bold and spicy flavors. Sichuan peppercorns, with their unique numbing sensation, are a hallmark of this region's cooking. One of the most celebrated dishes is Mapo Tofu, a spicy and aromatic dish featuring soft tofu cubes in a rich, chili-infused sauce with minced pork. The combination of the fiery heat from the chili bean paste and the tingling sensation from the peppercorns creates a complex and addictive flavor profile. Another staple is Kung Pao Chicken, a stir-fry of diced chicken, peanuts, and vegetables in a savory and slightly sweet sauce, often finished with a generous amount of dried red chilies.

Heading east to the coastal city of Shanghai, the cuisine takes on a more refined and delicate character. Known for its use of fresh, seasonal ingredients and a preference for sweet and savory flavors, Shanghai cuisine is exemplified by dishes like Xiaolongbao, or soup dumplings. These delicate dumplings are filled with a rich pork or crab filling and savory broth, requiring skillful handling to avoid breaking the thin dough skin. Another iconic dish is Red-Braised Pork Belly, a slow-cooked dish where pork belly is simmered in a mixture of soy sauce, sugar, and Shaoxing wine until it becomes tender and caramelized, resulting in a luxurious and flavorful dish.

In the southern province of Guangdong, Cantonese cuisine reigns supreme, characterized by its emphasis on fresh ingredients and subtle flavors. Dim sum, a collection of bite-sized dishes traditionally enjoyed during brunch, is perhaps the most well-known aspect of Cantonese cuisine. This tradition includes a wide variety of steamed and fried dumplings, buns, and rolls, each meticulously crafted to highlight the natural flavors of the ingredients. Har Gow, shrimp dumplings with a translucent wrapper, and Siu Mai, open-faced pork and shrimp dumplings, are perennial favorites. Another standout is Char Siu, Cantonese-style barbecued pork, marinated in a sweet and savory sauce and roasted until it achieves a perfect balance of caramelized exterior and juicy interior.

Moving to the west, the province of Yunnan offers a cuisine that is as diverse as its landscape, with influences from neighboring Southeast Asian countries. Yunnan is known for its use of wild mushrooms, fresh herbs, and a variety of spices. One of the most distinctive dishes from this region is Crossing the Bridge Noodles, a comforting and aromatic noodle soup served with a variety of raw and cooked ingredients that are added to the broth just before eating. The story behind the name is as charming as the dish itself, involving a devoted wife who would cross a bridge every day to bring her scholar husband his lunch, ensuring the ingredients remained hot and fresh by separating them until the last moment.

In the central province of Hunan, the cuisine is famous for its bold, spicy flavors and liberal use of chili peppers. Unlike Sichuan cuisine, which often employs the numbing heat of Sichuan peppercorns, Hunan dishes rely on the direct heat of fresh and dried chilies. One signature dish is Chairman Mao's Red-Braised Pork, named after Mao Zedong, who hailed from this region. This dish features succulent pieces of pork belly braised in a rich sauce made from soy sauce, sugar, and spices, resulting in a dish that is both sweet and spicy. Another popular dish is Dry Pot Chicken, where chicken pieces are stir-fried with an array of vegetables and spices in a sizzling hot pot, creating a dish that is intensely flavorful and satisfying.

Venturing to the northeast, the cuisine of Dongbei (Northeast China) is hearty and robust, reflecting the region's cold climate. Here, wheat-based staples like noodles and dumplings play a central role in the diet. One of the most beloved dishes is Dongbei Dumplings, which are typically filled with pork, cabbage, and chives, and served with a tangy dipping sauce made from vinegar and garlic. Another staple is Guo Bao Rou, a sweet and sour pork dish where thin slices of pork are battered and fried until crispy, then coated in a sticky sauce made from sugar and vinegar. This dish is a testament to the region's ability to create comfort food that is both satisfying and deeply flavorful.

The island province of Hainan, located in the south, offers a cuisine that is light, fresh, and heavily influenced by its tropical climate. Hainanese Chicken Rice is perhaps the most famous export from this region, consisting of poached chicken served with fragrant rice cooked in chicken broth, along with a trio of dipping sauces: ginger paste, chili sauce, and soy sauce. The simplicity of the dish belies the skill required to achieve the perfect balance of flavors and textures, making it a beloved favorite both in China and abroad.

In the northwest, the cuisine of Xinjiang is influenced by the region's large Muslim population and its location along the ancient Silk Road. Xinjiang dishes often feature lamb, mutton, and a variety of spices that reflect the area's historical connections with Central Asia. A standout dish is Yang Rou Chuan, or lamb skewers, which are marinated in a mixture of cumin, chili, and other spices before being grilled over an open flame. The result is a smoky, flavorful skewer that is both tender and aromatic. Another popular dish is Da Pan Ji, or Big Plate Chicken, a hearty stew of chicken, potatoes, and bell peppers simmered in a spicy sauce, often served with wide, hand-pulled noodles to soak up the rich broth.

Indian Spices: A Symphony of Flavors

Indian cuisine is a vibrant tapestry woven from an array of spices, each contributing to the symphony of flavors that define the country's diverse culinary heritage. The use of spices in India goes beyond mere seasoning; it is an art form, a tradition, and a science. From the fiery heat of red chilies to the subtle sweetness of cardamom, spices are integral to the Indian culinary experience, transforming simple ingredients into extraordinary dishes. This chapter explores the essential spices of Indian cuisine, their unique characteristics, and how they are expertly combined to create dishes that are both flavorful and aromatic.

One cannot speak of Indian spices without first mentioning cumin, one of the most widely used spices in Indian cooking. Cumin seeds, with their warm, earthy flavor, are often dry-roasted to enhance their aroma before being ground into a fine powder. This spice is a key component in various spice blends, such as garam masala and curry powders, and is used in dishes ranging from dals (lentil soups) to curries and vegetable preparations. The distinct taste of cumin provides a robust foundation, balancing the heat and tanginess of other spices.

Turmeric, with its vibrant yellow hue and mild, slightly bitter flavor, is another cornerstone of Indian cuisine. Known for its anti-inflammatory properties and health benefits, turmeric is used in both fresh and dried forms. It imparts a golden color to dishes and is essential in many curries and rice preparations. Turmeric's subtle flavor pairs well with other spices, enhancing the complexity of the overall dish without overpowering it.

Coriander seeds, with their citrusy and slightly sweet flavor, are used whole or ground in numerous Indian dishes. The seeds are often dry-roasted to bring out their full aroma before being ground into a powder. Coriander is a key ingredient in spice blends and is used to flavor meats, vegetables, and legumes. The fresh leaves of the coriander plant, known as cilantro, are also widely used as a garnish and flavor enhancer, adding a fresh and herbal note to dishes.

The intense heat of red chilies is a defining characteristic of many Indian dishes. Dried red chilies are used whole, crushed, or ground into powder, providing varying levels of heat and flavor. Kashmiri red chili powder, known for its vibrant red color and moderate heat, is often used to add both color and flavor to dishes without overwhelming them with spiciness. In contrast, the fiery heat of bird's eye chilies is reserved for those who enjoy a more intense kick. The careful balance of chili heat is crucial in Indian cooking, ensuring that the spice enhances rather than masks the flavors of other ingredients.

Fenugreek seeds, with their slightly bitter and nutty flavor, are another essential spice in Indian cuisine. These small, yellow seeds are often used in spice blends and pickles, lending a distinctive taste to dishes. Fenugreek leaves, known as methi, are also used fresh or dried to add a subtle bitterness and depth of flavor to curries and vegetable dishes. The versatility of fenugreek makes it a valuable addition to the Indian spice repertoire.

Mustard seeds, available in black, brown, and yellow varieties, are a staple in Indian cooking. The seeds are often tempered in hot oil until they pop, releasing their pungent and nutty aroma. This technique, known as tadka or tempering, is used to flavor dals, curries, and vegetable dishes, adding a layer of complexity to the final dish. Mustard seeds are also used in pickling, where their sharp flavor enhances the tanginess of pickled vegetables.

Cardamom, with its sweet, floral aroma and flavor, is a spice that adds a touch of elegance to both savory and sweet dishes. Green cardamom pods are used whole or ground, imparting a delicate fragrance to biryanis, curries, and desserts. Black cardamom, with its smoky and bold flavor, is typically used in savory dishes, adding depth and warmth. The versatility of cardamom makes it an indispensable spice in the Indian kitchen.

Cloves, with their strong, sweet, and slightly bitter flavor, are another spice that plays a significant role in Indian cuisine. These dried flower buds are used whole or ground to flavor rice dishes, meat curries, and spice blends. The intense aroma of cloves adds a warm and spicy note to dishes, complementing other spices like cinnamon and cardamom.

Cinnamon, known for its sweet and woody flavor, is a spice that adds warmth and depth to Indian dishes. Cinnamon sticks are often used in biryanis and pilafs, while ground cinnamon is incorporated into spice blends and desserts. The subtle sweetness of cinnamon balances the heat and acidity of other spices, creating a harmonious flavor profile.

Bay leaves, with their mild and slightly floral flavor, are used to infuse dishes with a subtle aroma. Indian bay leaves, also known as tej patta, are different from Mediterranean bay leaves and have a distinct flavor profile. They are typically used whole in rice dishes, curries, and stews, imparting a gentle fragrance that enhances the overall dish without overpowering it.

Asafoetida, known as hing, is a pungent spice derived from the resin of the ferula plant. Despite its strong and unpleasant smell in raw form, asafoetida transforms into a flavor enhancer when cooked, adding a savory and umami note to dishes. It is commonly used in vegetarian dishes, particularly in lentil soups and vegetable curries, where it substitutes for the flavors of garlic and onion.

The art of blending spices is what sets Indian cuisine apart, creating layers of flavor that tantalize the taste buds. Garam masala, a traditional spice blend, varies from region to region and even from household to household. Typically made from a combination of cumin, coriander, cardamom, cloves, cinnamon, and black pepper, garam masala is added towards the end of cooking to preserve its aromatic qualities. This blend adds warmth and depth to dishes, enhancing their overall flavor.

Another quintessential spice blend is curry powder, a mix of turmeric, cumin, coriander, fenugreek, and red chili powder. While not traditionally Indian, curry powder has become synonymous with Indian cuisine in the West. Each family or region might have its own variation, adjusting the proportions and types of spices to suit their taste.

Beyond these basics, regional variations in spice usage lead to an even broader spectrum of flavors. In the southern states, for example, coconut and tamarind are often used alongside spices to create tangy and rich curries. In contrast, the cuisine of Rajasthan, influenced by its arid climate, often features dried mango powder and kachri, a wild cucumber, to add sourness and depth.

The significance of spices in Indian cuisine extends beyond their flavor. They are also valued for their medicinal properties. Turmeric, for instance, is known for its anti-inflammatory and antioxidant benefits. Cumin aids in digestion, while cardamom is believed to help with respiratory ailments. This traditional knowledge of the health benefits of spices has been passed down through generations, further enriching the culinary heritage of India.

Mastering the use of Indian spices requires an understanding of their individual characteristics and how they interact with each other. It involves knowing when to add each spice during the cooking process to maximize its flavor potential. For example, whole spices are often tempered in oil at the beginning of cooking to release their essential oils, while ground spices might be added later to preserve their potency.

For beginners, starting with simple recipes and gradually experimenting with different combinations of spices can be a rewarding journey. Using pre-made spice blends can be a helpful shortcut, but nothing compares to the aroma and flavor of freshly ground spices. Investing in a good spice grinder and sourcing high-quality spices can make a significant difference in the outcome of your dishes.

Thai Cuisine: Balancing Sweet, Sour, Spicy, and Salty

The essence of Thai cuisine lies in its masterful balance of sweet, sour, spicy, and salty flavors. This intricate harmony is what makes Thai food so appealing and memorable. Each dish is crafted to excite the palate, offering a burst of contrasting flavors that come together in perfect unity. This chapter explores the foundational elements of Thai cuisine, delving into the key ingredients, cooking techniques, and iconic dishes that exemplify this culinary art.

Thai cuisine is deeply influenced by the geography and climate of Thailand, a tropical country abundant in fresh produce, herbs, and seafood. The use of fresh ingredients is paramount, with herbs like cilantro, basil, and mint playing crucial roles in flavor profiles. Vegetables such as lemongrass, galangal, and kaffir lime leaves add aromatic complexity, while ingredients like fish sauce and shrimp paste provide the umami depth that complements the other flavors.

One cannot discuss Thai cuisine without mentioning the ubiquitous presence of fish sauce. This fermented condiment, made from anchovies and salt, is a cornerstone of Thai cooking. It imparts a salty, savory depth to dishes, much like soy sauce does in Chinese cuisine. Fish sauce is used in everything from soups and curries to salads and dipping sauces, often combined with lime juice, sugar, and chilies to create a balanced dressing or marinade.

Another essential ingredient is palm sugar, derived from the sap of palm trees. It has a rich, caramel-like sweetness that is less intense than refined sugar, making it perfect for balancing the spicy and sour elements in Thai dishes. Palm sugar is often used in curries, desserts, and beverages, adding a subtle sweetness that enhances the overall flavor profile.

Chilies are integral to Thai cuisine, providing the characteristic heat that many dishes are known for. Thai cuisine uses a variety of chilies, from the mild prik chi fa to the fiery bird's eye chili. The level of spiciness can vary significantly, but the goal is always to achieve a balance with the other flavors. For instance, the heat of chilies is often tempered by the sweetness of palm sugar or the sourness of lime juice.

Lime juice is another key player, adding a bright and tangy acidity that lifts the flavors of a dish. Freshly squeezed lime juice is preferred, as it provides a vibrant sourness that cannot be replicated by bottled alternatives. Lime juice is a common ingredient in salads, soups, and dipping sauces, where it balances the saltiness of fish sauce and the heat of chilies.

Coconut milk, with its rich and creamy texture, is used extensively in Thai curries and desserts. It adds a luxurious mouthfeel and a subtle sweetness that balances the spiciness of curry pastes. Made by grating the flesh of mature coconuts and soaking it in hot water, coconut milk is an essential ingredient in dishes like green curry, massaman curry, and tom kha gai (chicken coconut soup).

Thai cooking is also characterized by the use of fresh herbs, which add brightness and complexity to dishes. Thai basil, with its anise-like flavor, is commonly used in stir-fries and curries. Cilantro, both the leaves and roots, is used as a garnish and in marinades. Mint leaves are often added to salads and appetizers, providing a refreshing contrast to the other flavors.

One of the most iconic Thai dishes is tom yum goong, a hot and sour soup that perfectly exemplifies the balance of flavors in Thai cuisine. This soup is made with shrimp, mushrooms, lemongrass, galangal, kaffir lime leaves, and chilies, all simmered in a broth flavored with fish sauce and lime juice. The result is a complex and aromatic soup that is simultaneously spicy, sour, and savory, with a hint of sweetness from the shrimp.

Green curry, or kaeng khiao wan, is another classic dish that showcases the rich and vibrant flavors of Thai cuisine. Made with green curry paste, coconut milk, and a variety of vegetables and proteins, this curry is known for its bright green color and intense flavor. The green curry paste, made from fresh green chilies, lemongrass, galangal, and other herbs, provides a spicy and aromatic base, while the coconut milk adds creaminess and sweetness.

Pad Thai, perhaps the most famous Thai dish outside of Thailand, is a stir-fried noodle dish that balances sweet, sour, spicy, and salty flavors in a single plate. Made with rice noodles, tofu or shrimp, eggs, bean sprouts, and peanuts, Pad Thai is flavored with tamarind paste, fish sauce, palm sugar, and chilies. The result is a dish that is both satisfying and complex, with a delightful interplay of textures and flavors.

Som tam, or green papaya salad, is a refreshing and spicy salad that is a staple of Thai street food. Made with shredded green papaya, tomatoes, green beans, and peanuts, the salad is dressed with a mixture of fish sauce, lime juice, palm sugar, and chilies. The crisp and crunchy texture of the papaya, combined with the bold flavors of the dressing, makes som tam a perfect example of the balance of flavors in Thai cuisine.

Another beloved dish is massaman curry, a rich and hearty curry that reflects the influence of Indian and Persian cuisines on Thai cooking. Made with massaman curry paste, coconut milk, potatoes, and peanuts, this curry has a unique flavor profile that combines the sweet, spicy, and tangy elements of Thai cuisine with the warm spices of Indian cooking. The result is a dish that is both comforting and complex, with layers of flavor that unfold with each bite.

Thai cuisine also includes a variety of refreshing beverages and desserts that balance the spicy and savory dishes. Thai iced tea, made with strong black tea, sugar, and condensed milk, is a sweet and creamy drink that provides a cooling contrast to the heat of Thai food. Mango sticky rice, a popular dessert made with glutinous rice, coconut milk, and ripe mangoes, offers a delightful combination of sweet, creamy, and fruity flavors.

The cooking techniques in Thai cuisine are as varied as the flavors, ranging from stir-frying and grilling to steaming and slow-cooking. Stir-frying is a common method, particularly for noodle dishes and stir-fried vegetables, where ingredients are quickly cooked over high heat to preserve their texture and flavor.

Grilling is often used for meats and seafood, imparting a smoky flavor that complements the bold spices and marinades.

Steaming is another important technique, used for dishes like fish and dumplings, where the gentle cooking method allows the delicate flavors of the ingredients to shine. Slow-cooking is used for curries and braises, allowing the spices and aromatics to meld together and create a rich and complex flavor.

The art of balancing flavors in Thai cuisine is a skill that requires practice and intuition. It involves tasting and adjusting, adding a bit more lime juice for acidity, a touch of palm sugar for sweetness, or a dash of fish sauce for saltiness. This process is what makes Thai cooking so dynamic and exciting, as each dish can be tailored to suit individual preferences and tastes.

For beginners, starting with simple recipes and gradually experimenting with different combinations of flavors can be a rewarding journey. Understanding the role of each ingredient and how they interact with each other is key to mastering Thai cuisine. Freshness is paramount, so sourcing high-quality ingredients and herbs can make a significant difference in the final dish.

Korean BBQ and Kimchi: A Flavor Explosion

The allure of Korean BBQ and kimchi lies in their bold, vibrant flavors that captivate the senses and offer a uniquely interactive dining experience. Korean BBQ, known as "gogi-gui," involves grilling meat, typically beef, pork, or chicken, at the table, allowing diners to cook their food to their preferred level of doneness. This method of dining is not only a feast for the palate but also a social experience, bringing people together around a communal grill.

The key to a successful Korean BBQ lies in the quality of the meat and the marinades. Beef is often the star, with cuts like ribeye, short ribs, and brisket being particularly popular. "Bulgogi," which means "fire meat," is a well-known dish made from thinly sliced ribeye marinated in a mixture of soy sauce, sugar, sesame oil, garlic, and other seasonings. This marinade not only tenderizes the meat but also infuses it with a sweet and savory flavor that caramelizes beautifully on the grill.

Pork belly, or "samgyeopsal," is another favorite in Korean BBQ. Unlike beef, pork belly is typically not marinated but seasoned lightly with salt before grilling. The high-fat content of pork belly makes it incredibly rich and flavorful, with a crispy exterior and a juicy interior when grilled to perfection. It is often served with "ssamjang," a thick, spicy dipping sauce made from fermented soybean paste, chili paste, garlic, and sesame oil.

Chicken, though less traditional, is also a popular choice for Korean BBQ. "Dak galbi" is a marinated chicken dish that includes gochujang, a fermented red chili paste that is a staple in Korean cuisine. The gochujang imparts a deep, spicy flavor to the chicken, which is often grilled with vegetables like sweet potatoes, carrots, and cabbage.

Vegetables play a crucial role in balancing the rich, fatty flavors of the grilled meats. Common accompaniments include lettuce leaves, which are used to wrap pieces of meat along with rice, garlic, and ssamjang. This practice, known as "ssam," adds a refreshing crunch and a burst of flavor with every bite. Other popular side dishes, or "banchan," include kimchi, pickled radishes, and seasoned spinach, all of which provide a variety of textures and flavors that complement the grilled meats.

Kimchi, perhaps the most iconic Korean dish, is a fermented vegetable dish that is both a staple and a symbol of Korean cuisine. While napa cabbage kimchi is the most well-known, there are countless varieties made with different vegetables, such as radish, cucumber, and green onion. The fermentation process not only preserves the vegetables but also develops a complex flavor profile that is tangy, spicy, and umami-rich.

Making kimchi involves several steps, starting with salting the vegetables to draw out moisture and create the right texture for fermentation. The vegetables are then mixed with a paste made from gochugaru (Korean red chili powder), garlic, ginger, fish sauce, and sometimes shrimp paste. This mixture is packed tightly into jars and left to ferment at room temperature before being moved to a cooler environment for long-term storage. The length of fermentation can vary, with kimchi becoming more sour and complex over time.

Kimchi is not only a side dish but also a versatile ingredient that can be used in a variety of recipes. Kimchi jjigae, a spicy kimchi stew, is a comforting dish made with aged kimchi, tofu, pork, and other ingredients. The fermentation process of the kimchi adds a depth of flavor to the stew that is both hearty and satisfying. Kimchi pancakes, or "kimchijeon," are another popular dish, made by mixing chopped kimchi with a simple batter of flour and water before frying to a crispy perfection.

The health benefits of kimchi are well-documented. Rich in probiotics due to the fermentation process, kimchi promotes gut health and aids digestion. It is also packed with vitamins A, B, and C, as well as fiber and antioxidants, making it a nutritious addition to any meal.

One cannot overlook the importance of sauces in Korean BBQ. Ssamjang and gochujang are staples, but there are also lighter, more refreshing sauces like "pa muchim," a seasoned green onion salad. This simple mixture of green onions, sesame oil, soy sauce, and chili flakes adds a bright, tangy counterpoint to the rich grilled meats. Another popular condiment is "chogochujang," a sweet and sour dipping sauce made from gochujang, vinegar, and sugar, often served with raw or lightly blanched seafood.

Rice is a fundamental component of Korean BBQ and meals in general. Short-grain white rice, known for its sticky texture, is the most common, though multigrain rice or "japgokbap" is also popular. The rice serves as a neutral base that balances the intense flavors of the meat and banchan, providing a harmonious dining experience.

The tradition of Korean BBQ extends beyond the food itself to the etiquette and customs surrounding it. Sharing food is a key aspect of Korean culture, and Korean BBQ embodies this spirit of communal dining. It is customary for diners to cook for each other, ensuring that everyone at the table enjoys perfectly grilled meat. Additionally, respect for elders is paramount; younger diners will often serve the older members of the group first, reflecting the deep-rooted values of Korean society.

For those new to Korean BBQ and kimchi, it can be helpful to start with a few basic recipes and gradually explore more complex dishes. Bulgogi and samgyeopsal are excellent starting points, as they are relatively straightforward and showcase the fundamental flavors of Korean BBQ. Making kimchi at home can be a rewarding experience, allowing you to experiment with different vegetables and fermentation times to find your preferred taste.

When preparing Korean BBQ at home, having the right equipment can make a significant difference. A tabletop grill or a portable gas burner with a grill plate is ideal for replicating the authentic experience. Additionally, investing in high-quality ingredients, such as well-marbled beef and fresh vegetables, will elevate the overall meal.

Chapter 4

Middle Eastern Feasts

Persian Cuisine: A Rich Heritage

Persian cuisine offers a tantalizing glimpse into a rich cultural heritage that spans thousands of years. Known for its intricate flavors and aromatic dishes, Persian food reflects the diverse geography and history of Iran. The cuisine is characterized by the use of fresh herbs, distinctive spices, and a balance of sweet and sour tastes. Central to Persian cooking are rice dishes, stews, kebabs, and an array of appetizers and desserts, each with its own unique preparation methods and historical significance.

Rice, or "chelow," is a cornerstone of Persian cuisine and is often served with every meal. The preparation of rice is an art form, with techniques passed down through generations. One of the most revered rice dishes is "tahdig," which translates to "bottom of the pot." Tahdig is the crispy, golden layer of rice that forms at the bottom of the pot during cooking. Achieving the perfect tahdig requires skill and patience, as the rice must be cooked just right to develop a crunchy crust without burning. This prized component is often served as a special treat at the beginning of the meal.

Another iconic rice dish is "zereshk polo," which features saffron-infused rice mixed with barberries and slivered almonds. The tartness of the barberries contrasts beautifully with the aromatic saffron, creating a harmonious blend of flavors. This dish is typically served with chicken or lamb, making it a popular choice for festive occasions and family gatherings.

Stews, or "khoresh," are another fundamental aspect of Persian cuisine. These slow-cooked dishes are known for their depth of flavor and comforting qualities. One of the most beloved stews is "fesenjan," a rich and tangy concoction made with ground walnuts and pomegranate molasses. The combination of these ingredients results in a luscious, dark sauce that envelops tender pieces of chicken or duck. The sweet and sour notes of fesenjan are a testament to the Persian palate's love for balanced flavors.

"Ghormeh sabzi" is another classic stew, celebrated for its vibrant green color and herbaceous flavor. This dish is made with a mixture of sautéed herbs, including parsley, cilantro, and fenugreek, along with kidney beans and chunks of meat, usually lamb or beef. Dried limes, or "limoo amani," are added to the stew, imparting a unique, slightly bitter citrus flavor that enhances the overall complexity of the dish.

Ghormeh sabzi is often served with rice, making it a hearty and satisfying meal.

Kebabs, or "kabab," hold a special place in Persian cuisine and are often associated with festive occasions and outdoor gatherings. The variety of kebabs is extensive, ranging from "kabab koobideh," made with seasoned ground meat, to "kabab barg," which features marinated lamb or beef. The meat is typically marinated in a mixture of yogurt, saffron, onions, and spices, which tenderizes the meat and infuses it with flavor. Grilling the kebabs over an open flame adds a smoky char that enhances the taste and texture.

One of the most visually striking and flavorful kebabs is "joojeh kabab," which consists of saffron-marinated chicken skewers. The bright yellow hue of the chicken, achieved through the use of saffron, turmeric, and lemon juice, makes this dish as appealing to the eyes as it is to the palate. Joojeh kabab is often served with grilled tomatoes and bell peppers, along with a side of saffron rice or flatbread.

Appetizers, or "meze," play a significant role in Persian dining, offering a variety of small dishes that are perfect for sharing. "Mirza ghasemi," a smoky eggplant dip, is a popular choice, made by charring eggplants over an open flame and mixing them with tomatoes, garlic, and eggs. The result is a rich, velvety spread that pairs wonderfully with fresh flatbread.

"Borani," a yogurt-based dip mixed with spinach or eggplant, is another common appetizer, providing a refreshing contrast to the more robust flavors of the main dishes. The use of yogurt in Persian cuisine is widespread, not only for its cooling properties but also for its ability to enhance the flavor and texture of dishes. "Mast-o khiar," a simple yet delicious yogurt and cucumber dip, is often seasoned with mint and dried rose petals, creating a delightful blend of flavors that can be enjoyed as a starter or side dish.

Desserts in Persian cuisine are a celebration of sweetness and fragrance, often incorporating ingredients like rose water, saffron, and cardamom. "Sholeh zard," a saffron rice pudding, is a traditional dessert that is both visually stunning and delectable. The bright yellow color of the pudding comes from saffron, while the rose water and cardamom add a floral and spicy aroma. Topped with slivered almonds and cinnamon, sholeh zard is a treat for both the eyes and the taste buds.

"Baghlava," the Persian version of baklava, is another beloved dessert, featuring layers of flaky pastry, ground nuts, and a sweet syrup flavored with rose water and cardamom. This rich and indulgent dessert is often enjoyed with a cup of Persian tea, which is typically brewed strong and served with a touch of sugar.

The cultural significance of Persian cuisine extends beyond the food itself to the customs and traditions surrounding it. Hospitality is a central tenet of Persian culture, and sharing food is a way of expressing generosity and warmth. When invited to a Persian home, guests are often greeted with an array of dishes, reflecting the host's desire to offer the best of what they have. This tradition of hospitality is deeply ingrained in Persian society and is evident in the care and attention given to the preparation and presentation of meals.

Persian cuisine also reflects the country's diverse climate and geography, which have influenced the ingredients and cooking methods used in different regions. The northern provinces, with their lush landscapes and access to the Caspian Sea, are known for dishes that feature fresh herbs, fish, and rice. In contrast, the more arid regions of central and southern Iran rely on ingredients like dates, nuts, and spices to create flavorful and sustaining dishes.

The historical influences on Persian cuisine are equally significant. Over the centuries, Persian cooking has been shaped by interactions with neighboring cultures, including the Greeks, Arabs, Turks, and Mongols. These exchanges have enriched Persian cuisine, introducing new ingredients and techniques that have been adapted and integrated into the culinary tradition.

Lebanese Mezze: A Table of Small Delights

Lebanese mezze, a vibrant and varied selection of small dishes, represents the heart of Lebanese cuisine. This delightful spread, often enjoyed with family and friends, offers a rich tapestry of flavors and textures that can turn any meal into a festive occasion. Mezze is not just about the food; it's about the experience of sharing, conversation, and conviviality. Each dish, from the simplest dip to the most elaborate preparation, tells a story of tradition, culture, and culinary artistry.

The concept of mezze revolves around a collection of appetizers that can be served as a starter or as a complete meal. The variety is immense, catering to all tastes, whether you prefer vegetarian, meat, or seafood dishes. Hummus, perhaps the most famous of all Lebanese dishes, is a creamy blend of chickpeas, tahini, lemon juice, and garlic. This humble dip, often garnished with a drizzle of olive oil and a sprinkle of paprika or fresh parsley, is both nutritious and delicious. It is typically scooped up with pieces of warm pita bread, making it a perfect start to the mezze experience.

Another staple of Lebanese mezze is baba ghanoush, a smoky eggplant dip that rivals hummus in popularity. The eggplants are charred over an open flame to impart a deep, smoky flavor, then blended with tahini, garlic, lemon juice, and olive oil. The result is a luscious, silky dip that pairs beautifully with fresh vegetables or pita bread. The smokiness of baba ghanoush adds a unique depth to the mezze table, contrasting with the bright and tangy flavors of other dishes.

Tabbouleh, a refreshing salad made with finely chopped parsley, mint, tomatoes, onions, and bulgur wheat, is another essential component of Lebanese mezze. Dressed with olive oil and lemon juice, tabbouleh is light, zesty, and packed with fresh, vibrant flavors. The high ratio of herbs to bulgur sets Lebanese tabbouleh apart from other variations, making it a refreshing palate cleanser amidst richer dishes.

Fattoush, another beloved salad, combines crisp lettuce, tomatoes, cucumbers, radishes, and fried pieces of pita bread, all tossed in a tangy sumac and lemon dressing. The fried pita adds a delightful crunch, while the sumac lends a slightly tart flavor that elevates the salad. Fattoush is a perfect example of how Lebanese cuisine makes use of simple, fresh ingredients to create dishes that are both satisfying and healthful.

Kibbeh, often referred to as the national dish of Lebanon, is a versatile and flavorful addition to the mezze table. The most common form of kibbeh is made with a mixture of ground lamb or beef, bulgur wheat, and spices, shaped into small torpedo-like patties and fried until golden brown. The crispy exterior gives way to a savory, spiced filling that is incredibly satisfying. There are also variations of kibbeh that are baked or served raw, showcasing the versatility of this beloved dish.

For those who enjoy seafood, mezze offers tantalizing options like grilled octopus, shrimp in garlic and lemon, and fish kibbeh. These dishes highlight the Mediterranean influence on Lebanese cuisine, with an emphasis on fresh, simple preparations that allow the natural flavors of the seafood to shine through. Grilled octopus, for example, is often marinated in olive oil, lemon juice, and herbs before being charred on the grill, resulting in a tender, flavorful dish that is both elegant and approachable.

No mezze spread would be complete without a selection of pickles and olives. Pickled turnips, cucumbers, and wild cucumbers (known as "mukhalal") add a briny, tangy contrast to the richness of other dishes. Olives, whether green, black, or mixed, are marinated in olive oil, garlic, and herbs, providing a burst of flavor with each bite.

These small, flavorful accompaniments enhance the overall mezze experience, offering a delightful counterpoint to the heartier dishes.

One of the joys of mezze is the sheer variety of dishes that can be included, allowing for endless combinations and variations. Stuffed grape leaves, known as "warak enab," are a popular choice, filled with a mixture of rice, pine nuts, and spices, and sometimes ground meat. These tender, flavorful rolls are often served cold, drizzled with olive oil and lemon juice, making them a refreshing addition to the mezze table.

Falafel, crispy chickpea fritters seasoned with herbs and spices, are another favorite. These golden-brown balls are typically served with tahini sauce, pickles, and fresh vegetables, either on their own or stuffed into pita bread for a delicious sandwich. The crunchy exterior and moist, flavorful interior of falafel make it a beloved street food and a staple of mezze.

Lebanese sausages, known as "makanek," are small, spicy sausages made with ground meat and a blend of aromatic spices. They are usually sautéed and served hot, often with a squeeze of lemon juice to brighten the flavors. The robust, savory taste of makanek adds a satisfying, meaty element to the mezze spread.

For those with a sweet tooth, mezze can also include a selection of desserts to round out the meal. Baklava, layers of phyllo pastry filled with chopped nuts and sweetened with honey or syrup, is a classic choice. The delicate, flaky pastry and rich, nutty filling make baklava a perfect end to a mezze feast. Another popular dessert is "knafeh," a sweet cheese pastry soaked in syrup and topped with crushed pistachios. The combination of crispy pastry, gooey cheese, and fragrant syrup is irresistible.

Lebanese mezze is more than just a collection of dishes; it is a way of life. The joy of mezze lies in the communal experience, the sharing of food and conversation, and the celebration of flavors and traditions. Each dish, whether simple or complex, contributes to a rich tapestry of tastes that reflect the diversity and vibrancy of Lebanese culture. By embracing the spirit of mezze, you can bring a taste of Lebanon into your home, creating memorable meals that are as much about the people you share them with as the food itself.

Incorporating mezze into your culinary repertoire is a rewarding journey that begins with understanding the essential components and the philosophy behind them. Start with a few basic dishes, like hummus and tabbouleh, and gradually expand your menu to include more elaborate preparations. Pay attention to the balance of flavors and textures, and don't be afraid to experiment with different combinations and presentations.

As you become more comfortable with the techniques and ingredients, you can start to personalize your mezze spread, adding your own twists and variations to traditional recipes. The beauty of mezze is its flexibility and adaptability, allowing you to create a unique dining experience that reflects your tastes and creativity.

Turkish Delights: From Kebab to Baklava

Turkish cuisine, with its rich history and diverse influences, offers a tantalizing array of flavors and textures. Among its most celebrated contributions are the dishes that fall under the umbrella of "Turkish delights"—an expansive category that ranges from savory kebabs to sweet baklava. These foods are not just meals but an embodiment of Turkey's cultural and culinary heritage. Each dish has its own story, steeped in tradition and shaped by centuries of interaction between different cultures and regions.

Kebabs are perhaps the most iconic of Turkish dishes. The term "kebab" itself encompasses a variety of preparations, primarily centered around grilled or skewered meats. One of the most famous is the döner kebab, which involves layers of marinated meat—typically lamb, beef, or chicken— stacked onto a vertical rotisserie and slowly cooked as it rotates. Thin slices of the outer layer are shaved off as it cooks, served either in pita bread as a sandwich or on a plate with rice and vegetables. The marinade, often a blend of yogurt, garlic, and spices, imbues the meat with a deep, savory flavor that is unmistakably Turkish.

Shish kebab, another popular variant, consists of chunks of meat threaded onto skewers and grilled. These kebabs are often marinated in a mixture of olive oil, lemon juice, and spices before grilling, which helps to tenderize the meat and infuse it with flavor. The result is juicy, flavorful meat that is slightly charred on the outside, offering a delightful contrast in textures. Shish kebabs can be made with lamb, beef, chicken, or even fish, making them versatile enough to please a wide range of palates.

Adana kebab, named after the city of Adana in southern Turkey, is a spicier version typically made with ground lamb or beef mixed with chili flakes and other spices. The meat is shaped onto flat metal skewers and grilled over an open flame. The heat of the chili flakes and the smoky flavor from the grill create a bold, intense taste that is a favorite among spice lovers. Adana kebabs are often served with a side of grilled vegetables and flatbread, making for a hearty and satisfying meal.

Kebabs are not just about meat, though. Vegetarians can enjoy a variety of vegetable kebabs, such as those made with eggplant, tomatoes, and peppers. These vegetable kebabs are often marinated in olive oil and herbs, then grilled to bring out their natural sweetness and enhance their flavors. The combination of charred, smoky vegetables with fresh herbs and spices offers a delicious and healthful alternative to meat-based kebabs.

Moving from savory to sweet, baklava stands out as one of the most beloved Turkish desserts. This rich, sweet pastry is made from layers of thin phyllo dough, filled with chopped nuts—usually pistachios, walnuts, or almonds—and sweetened with syrup or honey. The preparation of baklava is an art form in itself, requiring skill and patience to layer the dough and nuts evenly. Once baked, the pastry is soaked in a fragrant syrup, often flavored with rosewater or orange blossom water, which gives it a unique and irresistible aroma.

Baklava's origins are a subject of some debate, with various cultures claiming it as their own, but it is widely acknowledged that it reached its pinnacle in the kitchens of the Ottoman Empire. Today, baklava is enjoyed throughout Turkey and beyond, often served with a cup of strong Turkish coffee to balance its sweetness. The contrast between the crisp layers of pastry, the crunch of the nuts, and the sticky sweetness of the syrup creates a symphony of textures and flavors that is hard to resist.

Another popular Turkish dessert is künefe, a cheese-filled pastry soaked in sweet syrup. Künefe is made with thin strands of dough called kadayıf, which are layered with a mild, stretchy cheese such as mozzarella or a traditional Turkish cheese like künefe peyniri. The pastry is baked until golden and crispy, then drenched in a syrup made from sugar, water, and lemon juice. Often topped with a sprinkle of crushed pistachios, künefe is served hot, with the cheese inside melting into a gooey, delicious filling.

Turkish delight, or lokum, is another sweet treat that has captured the hearts of many. These gelatinous cubes are flavored with rosewater, lemon, or mastic, and often contain nuts such as pistachios or hazelnuts. The texture of Turkish delight is unique—soft and chewy, with a slight firmness that gives way to a melt-in-your-mouth sensation. Traditionally, lokum is dusted with powdered sugar to prevent the pieces from sticking together and to add a touch of sweetness.

Beyond desserts, Turkish cuisine offers a variety of savory pastries that are also considered delights. Börek, for example, is a savory pastry made from layers of thin dough filled with cheese, spinach, or minced meat. These pastries are baked until golden and crispy, and they can be enjoyed as a snack or a light meal. Börek comes in many forms, from large, pie-like versions to small, finger-sized rolls, each with its own unique filling and preparation method.

Another beloved pastry is gözleme, a thin, flatbread filled with various ingredients such as cheese, spinach, or spiced ground meat, then cooked on a griddle. Gözleme is often enjoyed as a street food, freshly made to order and served hot. The combination of the crispy, flaky bread with the savory filling makes it a satisfying and portable meal.

The diversity of Turkish delights extends to beverages as well. Turkish tea and coffee are integral parts of the culinary experience. Turkish tea, or çay, is often served in small, tulip-shaped glasses and enjoyed throughout the day. The tea is strong and typically served with sugar, though not with milk. Turkish coffee, on the other hand, is a rich, thick brew made by boiling finely ground coffee beans with water and sugar. It is traditionally served in small cups, often accompanied by a piece of Turkish delight.

The communal aspect of enjoying these delights cannot be overstated. In Turkey, meals are often social events, bringing together family and friends to share food and conversation. The sharing of kebabs, pastries, and sweets fosters a sense of togetherness and conviviality, reflecting the culture's deep-rooted values of hospitality and community.

To truly appreciate Turkish delights, it's important to embrace the experience as a whole. This means not just tasting the food, but also understanding the traditions and customs that surround it. Whether you're enjoying a kebab at a bustling street market, savoring a piece of baklava in a cozy café, or sipping Turkish tea with friends, you're participating in a rich culinary tradition that has been honed and celebrated over centuries.

For those new to Turkish cuisine, the journey begins with exploring the myriad of flavors and dishes that make up this diverse culinary landscape. Start with the basics—try making a simple shish kebab at home or bake a batch of baklava. As you become more comfortable with the ingredients and techniques, venture into more complex recipes and experiment with different variations. The beauty of Turkish cuisine lies in its balance of bold flavors and subtle nuances, its ability to be both hearty and delicate, and its celebration of both the familiar and the exotic.

Moroccan Tagines and Couscous

The vibrant, aromatic cuisine of Morocco is a feast for the senses, characterized by its use of spices, herbs, and fresh ingredients. Central to this culinary tradition are tagines and couscous, dishes that encapsulate the essence of Moroccan cooking. These dishes are more than just food; they are a representation of Morocco's rich cultural tapestry, influenced by Berber, Arab, Andalusian, and Mediterranean cuisines.

Tagine, a slow-cooked stew braised at low temperatures, takes its name from the earthenware pot in which it is cooked. This conical-lidded pot is designed to return condensed steam to the food, keeping it moist and tender. Tagines can be made with a variety of ingredients, including meats, poultry, fish, and vegetables. What sets a tagine apart is the harmonious blend of spices and flavors, often including a mix of sweet and savory elements.

One of the most classic tagines is the lamb and prune tagine. This dish features tender lamb cooked with prunes, almonds, and a medley of spices such as cinnamon, ginger, saffron, and turmeric. The slow cooking process allows the lamb to absorb the sweet and spicy flavors, resulting in a rich, complex dish that is both hearty and elegant. The prunes add a natural sweetness that complements the savory lamb, while the almonds provide a satisfying crunch.

Chicken tagine with preserved lemons and olives is another quintessential Moroccan dish. This tagine combines the bright, tangy flavor of preserved lemons with the briny taste of green olives, creating a delicious contrast with the tender chicken. The dish is typically spiced with garlic, ginger, cumin, and coriander, and garnished with fresh cilantro. The preserved lemons, a staple in Moroccan cuisine, add a unique, intense citrus flavor that is hard to replicate with fresh lemons alone.

Vegetarian tagines are equally delightful and showcase the versatility of Moroccan cooking. A vegetable tagine might include a combination of carrots, potatoes, zucchini, and bell peppers, all simmered together with tomatoes, onions, garlic, and a blend of spices like cumin, paprika, and turmeric. The result is a colorful, flavorful dish that is both nourishing and satisfying. Adding chickpeas or lentils can boost the protein content, making the tagine a complete meal on its own.

Cooking a tagine requires a bit of patience and practice, but the results are well worth the effort. The key is to layer the ingredients properly in the tagine pot, starting with a bed of onions and garlic, followed by the main protein or vegetables, and finally the spices and liquid. The tagine is then covered and cooked slowly over low heat, allowing the flavors to meld together beautifully. If a traditional tagine pot is not available, a heavy-bottomed Dutch oven can be used as a substitute.

Couscous, often served as an accompaniment to tagines, is a staple in Moroccan cuisine. This tiny, granular pasta made from semolina wheat is incredibly versatile and can be prepared in various ways. Traditionally, couscous is steamed over a simmering pot of stew, which allows it to absorb the flavors of the dish. The grains become light and fluffy, a perfect base for the rich, saucy tagines.

A classic Moroccan couscous dish is couscous with seven vegetables. As the name suggests, it includes a variety of vegetables such as carrots, zucchini, turnips, pumpkin, cabbage, and chickpeas, cooked in a fragrant broth. The couscous is steamed in stages, starting with a light sprinkle of water and oil to prevent clumping. The vegetables and broth are then layered over the couscous, allowing it to soak up the flavors as it steams. The result is a beautifully aromatic and colorful dish that is both comforting and nutritious.

Another popular variation is couscous with lamb and vegetables, a hearty dish often prepared for special occasions. The lamb is cooked with spices like cumin, coriander, and saffron, along with a mix of vegetables such as carrots, potatoes, and zucchini. The resulting stew is served over a bed of fluffy couscous, garnished with fresh herbs and sometimes toasted almonds or raisins for added texture and flavor.

Sweet couscous dishes are also part of Moroccan cuisine, often served as a dessert or a special breakfast treat. One such dish is mesfouf, a sweet couscous flavored with orange blossom water, cinnamon, and powdered sugar, and topped with dried fruits and nuts. Another is seffa, a steamed couscous dish mixed with butter, sugar, and ground almonds, and often garnished with cinnamon and powdered sugar. These sweet variations highlight the versatility of couscous and its ability to adapt to different flavor profiles.

Preparing couscous from scratch can be a rewarding experience. While instant couscous is widely available and convenient, traditional steaming yields a superior texture and flavor. To prepare couscous traditionally, the grains are first moistened with water and oil, then rubbed between the hands to separate them. The couscous is then placed in a steamer basket (kesskess) over a pot of boiling water or stew and steamed in stages, with periodic fluffing to ensure even cooking. This method, though time-

consuming, results in light, airy couscous that
absorbs the flavors of the accompanying stew
perfectly.

The communal aspect of Moroccan dining is an
integral part of the experience. Meals are often
shared from a large, central dish, with family and
friends gathered around. This practice fosters a sense
of togetherness and connection, as everyone
partakes in the same meal. Eating with the hands,
using bread to scoop up food, is common and adds
to the intimate, communal feel of the meal.

To recreate the Moroccan dining experience at
home, consider serving tagines and couscous in
large, shared dishes. Accompany the meal with
traditional Moroccan bread, such as khobz, a round,
crusty bread perfect for dipping into the rich sauces.
Fresh salads, such as a simple tomato and cucumber
salad with mint, can provide a refreshing contrast to
the hearty tagines. Finish the meal with a pot of
Moroccan mint tea, a fragrant and soothing beverage
made with green tea, fresh mint leaves, and sugar.

For those new to Moroccan cuisine, starting with a
simple tagine and couscous dish can be an excellent
introduction. As you become more comfortable with
the ingredients and techniques, you can experiment

with different variations and flavors, exploring the rich diversity of Moroccan cooking. The key to mastering these dishes lies in the balance of flavors and the use of fresh, high-quality ingredients.

The beauty of Moroccan tagines and couscous lies in their ability to transform simple ingredients into extraordinary meals. The slow cooking process allows the flavors to develop and deepen, creating dishes that are rich, aromatic, and deeply satisfying. Whether you're enjoying a lamb tagine with prunes, a chicken tagine with preserved lemons, or a vegetable couscous, each bite is a journey through the vibrant culinary landscape of Morocco.

Israeli Innovations: Tradition Meets Modernity

Israeli cuisine is a captivating fusion of traditions, cultures, and flavors, reflecting the country's diverse population and rich history. At the heart of this culinary tapestry is a spirit of innovation, blending ancient recipes with modern techniques to create dishes that are both deeply rooted in tradition and refreshingly contemporary. This chapter delves into the innovative culinary landscape of Israel, exploring how traditional foods have been reimagined and new gastronomic trends have emerged.

One of the most iconic examples of Israeli culinary innovation is the elevation of falafel from a humble street food to a gourmet dish. Traditionally, falafel consists of deep-fried balls or patties made from ground chickpeas or fava beans, mixed with herbs and spices such as parsley, cumin, and coriander. Served in pita bread with fresh vegetables and tahini sauce, it has long been a staple of Middle Eastern cuisine. In recent years, Israeli chefs have experimented with this classic dish, introducing variations such as beetroot or sweet potato falafel, and serving it with sophisticated accompaniments like pickled vegetables, spicy harissa, and artisanal hummus.

Hummus, another beloved staple, has also undergone a remarkable transformation. While the traditional version, made from blended chickpeas, tahini, lemon juice, and garlic, remains a favorite, chefs have started to push the boundaries of this ancient dish. Creative variations include hummus with toppings like roasted pine nuts, spiced ground lamb, or sautéed mushrooms. Some versions incorporate unexpected ingredients, such as avocado or pumpkin, offering a fresh twist on the classic dip. These modern interpretations of hummus have not only revived interest in the dish but also highlighted its versatility and potential for innovation.

Shakshuka, a dish of poached eggs in a spicy tomato and pepper sauce, is another traditional favorite that has been reimagined in contemporary Israeli cuisine. While the original version is typically made with tomatoes, bell peppers, onions, and spices like cumin and paprika, modern renditions include variations with green tomatoes and spinach, or even with added cheese and sausage for a heartier meal. The adaptability of shakshuka has made it a popular choice for brunches and casual dining, showcasing the dynamic nature of Israeli culinary traditions.

Bread, a fundamental part of many cultures, holds a special place in Israeli cuisine as well. Challah, the traditional braided bread eaten on Shabbat and Jewish holidays, has seen numerous inventive variations. While the classic recipe calls for a slightly sweet, egg-enriched dough, modern bakers have experimented with different flavors and ingredients. Some versions include additions like chocolate chips, raisins, or even savory fillings such as pesto and sun-dried tomatoes. The creative reinterpretation of challah has breathed new life into this traditional bread, making it a versatile option for various occasions.

One cannot discuss Israeli culinary innovations without mentioning the thriving street food scene, which has become a canvas for culinary creativity. Sabich, a sandwich traditionally made with fried eggplant, hard-boiled eggs, hummus, tahini, and a variety of fresh vegetables, is a perfect example. Originally introduced by Iraqi Jews, this dish has been embraced and adapted by Israeli chefs. Modern versions might include grilled vegetables, different sauces, or even alternative protein sources like seitan or tofu, making it a versatile and inclusive option for various dietary preferences.

The influence of diverse immigrant communities on Israeli cuisine cannot be overstated. The influx of Jews from North Africa, Eastern Europe, and the Middle East has introduced a plethora of flavors and cooking techniques to the Israeli culinary landscape. For instance, Moroccan cuisine has contributed dishes like couscous and tagines, which have been integrated into Israeli cooking with local twists. Similarly, Eastern European immigrants have brought with them dishes like borscht and schnitzel, which have been adapted to include Israeli ingredients and flavors.

Israeli cuisine also embraces the concept of farm-to-table dining, with an emphasis on fresh, locally sourced ingredients. The country's Mediterranean climate provides an abundance of fresh produce, herbs, and spices, which are integral to its culinary identity. Farmers' markets, known as shuks, are central to this movement, offering a vibrant array of seasonal fruits and vegetables, as well as artisanal products like cheeses, olives, and bread. This focus on fresh, high-quality ingredients has inspired chefs to create dishes that highlight the natural flavors and beauty of the produce.

The culinary innovation in Israel extends to beverages as well. The country has a burgeoning wine industry, with vineyards producing high-quality wines that have gained international recognition. Israeli winemakers have embraced both traditional techniques and modern technology to craft wines that reflect the unique terroir of the region. Additionally, the craft beer scene in Israel has exploded in recent years, with microbreweries experimenting with local ingredients and flavors to create distinctive brews. This spirit of innovation is also evident in the growing popularity of craft cocktails, with bartenders incorporating local herbs, fruits, and spices into their creations.

Desserts in Israel have also seen a wave of innovation, blending traditional flavors with contemporary techniques. Malabi, a Middle Eastern milk pudding traditionally flavored with rose water and topped with syrup and nuts, has been reinterpreted in various ways. Modern versions might include flavors like cardamom, saffron, or even matcha, and are often garnished with fresh fruits, edible flowers, or exotic spices. Similarly, baklava, the rich, sweet pastry made with layers of filo dough, nuts, and honey, has been given new life with creative fillings such as pistachio and chocolate.

Israeli chefs are not only innovating within the framework of traditional dishes but are also pioneering new culinary concepts. The fusion of different cuisines and the incorporation of global influences have led to the creation of unique dishes that are distinctly Israeli yet globally inspired. This culinary experimentation is evident in the rise of fusion restaurants that blend elements of Middle Eastern, Mediterranean, Asian, and European cuisines, resulting in exciting and unexpected flavor combinations.

The culinary landscape of Israel is a testament to the dynamic interplay between tradition and modernity. By honoring their rich culinary heritage while embracing innovation and creativity, Israeli chefs have created a cuisine that is both deeply rooted in history and refreshingly contemporary. This balance of old and new, familiar and innovative, is what makes Israeli cuisine so captivating and delicious.

For those looking to explore Israeli culinary innovations at home, the key is to start with traditional recipes and then experiment with new ingredients and techniques. Whether it's adding a modern twist to a classic dish or creating something entirely new, the possibilities are endless. Embrace the spirit of innovation that defines Israeli cuisine, and let your creativity guide you in the kitchen.